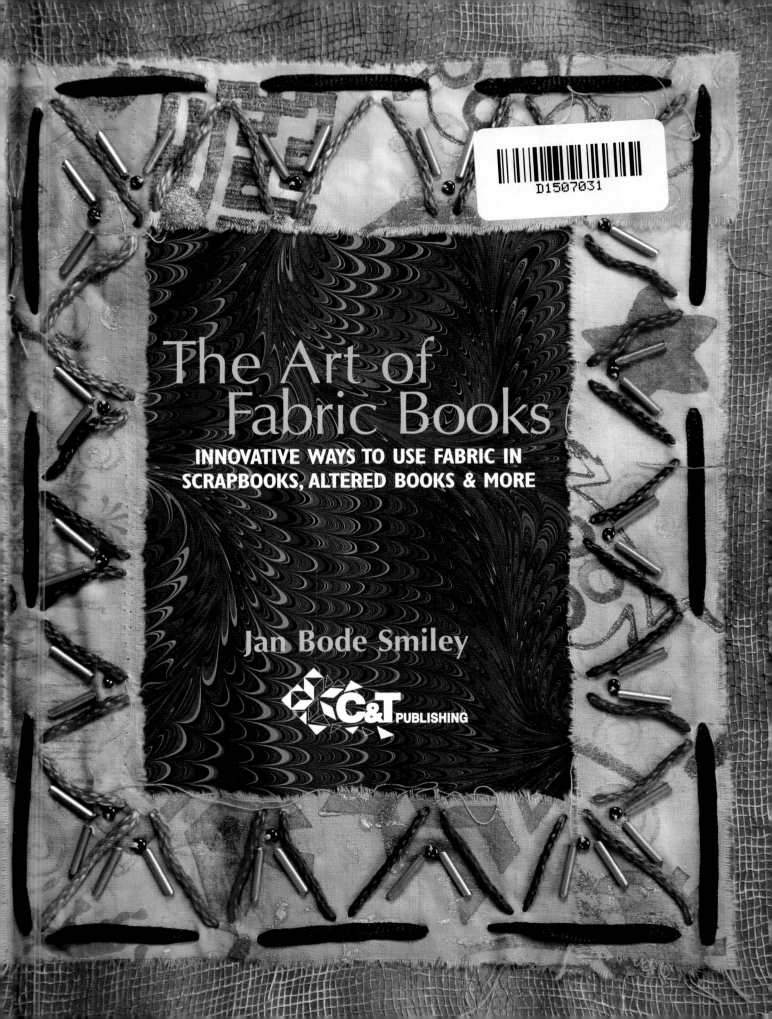

The Art of Fabric Books

INNOVATIVE WAYS TO USE FABRIC IN SCRAPBOOKS, ALTERED BOOKS & MORE

Jan Bode Smiley

C&T PUBLISHING

Text © 2005 Jan Bode Smiley
Artwork © 2005 C&T Publishing
Publisher: Amy Marson
Editorial Director: Gailen Runge
Acquistions Editor: Jan Grigsby
Editor: Liz Aneloski
Technical Editor: Sara Kate MacFarland
Copyeditors: Wordfirm/Stacy Chamness
Proofreader: Lori Erokan
Cover Designer: Christina Jarumay
Design Director/Book Designer: Kristen Yenche
Illustrator: Tim Manibusan
Production Assistant: Tim Manibusan
Photo Stylist: Diane Pedersen
Photography: Luke Mulks unless otherwise noted
Published by C&T Publishing, Inc., P.O. Box 1456, Lafayette,
California, 94549

Library of Congress Cataloging-in-Publication Data
Smiley, Jan Bode
  The art of fabric books : innovative ways to use fabric in scrapbooks,
altered books & more / Jan Smiley.
      p. cm.
  Includes bibliographical references and index.
  ISBN 1-57120-281-1 (paper trade)
  1. Altered books. 2. Scrapbooks. 3. Textile fabrics. I. Title.
  TT896.3.S53 2005
  746--dc22
2004010897

Printed in China
10 9 8 7 6 5 4 3 2 1

Dedication

I would like to dedicate this book to my family:

To Tom—thanks to his support, I am free to follow my muse.

To Emma—my most reliable walking partner and my best sounding board.

To Keith—for his daily reminders that there is much more to life than work.

Acknowledgments

Thanks to Jan, Liz, Diane, and the entire team at C&T for believing in me and making this book possible. Their professionalism is amazing and their successful teamwork shows in their incredible finished products. I am proud to associate with them.

Thanks to Kristi Steiner for checking in on me at just the right time, every time.

Thanks to the wonderful book artists who came through with inspiring work for the Gallery. Their artwork truly makes this book special and I appreciate their trust in me.

Thanks to the growing number of people who are also "crossing over" into other mediums. This is an exciting time. Quilters, book artists, painters, stampers, scrapbook artists, and crafters are discovering commonality that will enhance all our lives.

Table of Contents

Introduction

HISTORY OF ALTERED BOOKS AND SCRAPBOOKS

Did you scribble in a book when you were a child? Have you pasted photos, newspaper clippings, or favorite recipes onto another piece of paper? If you answered yes to either of these questions, you've already altered a book or started scrapbooking, even before you had a name to attach to it.

Although their current resurgence in popularity has drawn fresh attention to these art forms, they have been around since long before any of us were born. In 1769, James Granger's *Biographical History of England* included blank pages for the owner to insert his or her choice of illustrations.

In previous eras, paper was expensive and often scarce. Monks were known to scrape the old ink off a page to use the paper for new text and illustrations. In the Victorian era, old books were used as foundations for pasting items from magazines, photographs, and recipes.

SOME CLARIFICATIONS

What Is an Altered Book?

An altered book is any book that has been altered, or changed, in some way.

What Is a Fabric Book?

A fabric book is a constructed book made primarily of fabric. It didn't start out as a book structure but has been created to function like a book.

What Is a Fabric Altered Book?

A fabric altered book is an existing book that has been altered using fabric, sewing techniques, and notions in the altering process.

What Is an Altered Scrapbook?

An altered scrapbook serves the same purpose as a traditional scrapbook but may incorporate a wider variety of techniques and materials. Altered scrapbooks might be housed in an already existing book. In this case, there is a definite crossover between altered books and scrapbooks.

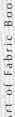

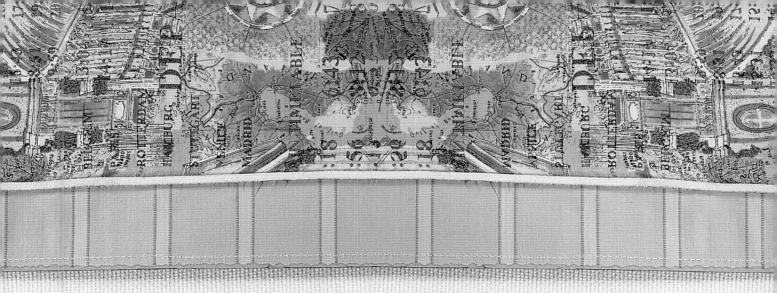

CROSSOVER

For example, the *My Aunt Gladys* book (pages 76–81) was created inside an old ledger book to honor her career as a bookkeeper. You could use a similar idea to honor a favorite teacher or course subject by altering a textbook and incorporating notes or grades from the class or memories of that experience.

How about using an out-of-date travel guide as your book base for creating a scrapbook about your (real or imagined!) trip? If you incorporate fabric or sewing techniques in the process, you are, in effect, creating an altered book, scrapbook, and fabric altered book all at the same time. Multi-tasking can be so much fun!

One of the fantastic things about this growing medium is the ability to incorporate any technique, material, or process that you want to employ to create your unique vision. This is a medium where the phrase "there are no rules" really is true. So grab your supplies and start exploring this exciting process!

WHAT DO I NEED TO GET STARTED?

Many items that are essential to these processes are already in your home, or can be acquired quickly and inexpensively. Although there are always new and exciting items that can be incorporated into your next work, you don't have to spend a lot of money *before* experimenting with the wonderful techniques in this book. After you get started on a project, you'll have a better idea of what items will be most useful for you; shopping at that point may be a better use of your time and money. With that said, there are a few essential items you need before you dive into your project.

To get started on a fabric book, you'll need some fabric. Some thread or glue to hold things together is pretty important, too.

To get started on a fabric altered book, you'll need a book and some fabric. Add glue or thread, and you're ready to go!

To get started on an altered book or a scrapbook, you'll need a book (blank or not—your choice), some memorabilia, and some thread and/or glue.

See? I told you that you already had the essentials at hand! Let's get moving!

How to Use This Book

This book is divided into several sections. The **Techniques** section will show you various ways to accomplish projects, such as framing images in your book projects, incorporating pockets onto your book page, or joining a section of pages together in an altered book.

The **Book Construction** section will show you the step-by-step processes for creating a tag book, a constructed fabric book, a fabric altered book, and a scrapbook, as well as some other fun book projects, and give you the guidance you need to create your own version.

The **Gallery** is sheer inspiration. I am pleased that these talented artists shared their work with us.

Throughout this book, we will explore ways to incorporate a variety of techniques and materials into your next scrapbook, altered book, or constructed fabric book project. Some of the materials and techniques may already be in your repertoire. Other products and processes may be new to you. We all have taken a unique creative path to come to this point in our lives, and here is our chance to combine past experiences, current skills, and newly acquired techniques in one powerful medium: the book.

If you are a quiltmaker, the fabrics, threads, and stitching techniques will be very familiar to you, but you may be new to stamping or paper art. If you are a rubber-stamp artist, the paper, inks, and stamps will be comfortable for you, but perhaps you have never worked with fabric or thread. If you are a writer, words may be your comfort zone, but perhaps you've never taken the opportunity to work creatively with your hands. It does not matter what your creative background or experience is—what matters is that *The Art of Fabric Books* is a place where we can join together and understand one another. The goal is to have fun and experiment with new ideas and materials.

So, grab a cup of coffee, find a comfy chair, and read as much or as little of this book as you want. If you get inspired right away, by all means, start creating, and read more later if you need more ideas. To plan ahead, make notes about certain techniques that you'd really like to try, and get started as soon as you have a plan.

We all approach *The Art of Fabric Books* with different experience levels and backgrounds, so I provide this section to ensure that we are all speaking the same language. Perhaps you've never been in an art supply store and are intimidated by the choices. If you have never made a scrapbook, you might not know what to look for when you enter a scrapbook store. Perhaps fabric tools are unfamiliar to you, and you hesitate to enter your nearest quilt shop. The intent of this chapter is to help you feel comfortable with the language and tools so you know what to look for when you are shopping.

Tip

Flannel-backed vinyl tablecloths from the dollar store make a great, reusable, "messy" surface underneath paper and fabric when you are painting.

TOOLS AND SUPPLIES
Acrylic Paint

Acrylic paints are wonderful for painting in books. They dry quickly, are safe to use, and are readily available. But be aware that when it comes to acrylic paints, you get what you pay for. The very inexpensive paints do not have much pigment or color in them. Instead, you are buying a lot of binder and not much color.

More expensive brands typically have more pigment in them; therefore, you can thin them with other materials without losing their intense color. My favorite brands are Jo Sonja's and Golden. My advice is to buy the best quality paint you can afford.

Tip Clean, empty glassine (waxy paper cereal bags), opened flat, make wonderful, disposable work surfaces behind any items you are painting. Open at the seam and use them to protect your work surface from paint and glues.

Adhesives

Oh, where to start? There are so many different adhesives!

Here are some basic guidelines for adhesives and the most appropriate uses for each of them. As you work, you'll decide which you prefer.

School Glue

The thought of white school glue may bring back memories of elementary school. Sometimes referred to as PVA (which stands for polyvinyl acetate), these water-based synthetic adhesives are easy-to-use, multipurpose glues. Some are acid free, so look for them if that is important to you. Otherwise, though the labeling and consistency of the glue varies, they all share the same basic recipe and should work well in your book projects.

Tools

Crafter's Pick White Glues

The Ultimate, Fabric Glue, and Memory Mount are all Crafter's Pick brand glues, though this company's line includes many more options as well.

These thick, white glues are nontoxic, water-based adhesives that dry clear. The Fabric Glue is specifically formulated for fabric and is washable. The Ultimate is great for adhering heavier items in your books. Memory Mount is acid free. They all dry fairly quickly and are very versatile. These are my all-around favorite white glues.

Double-Stick Tape

For lightweight paper items, double-stick tape is handy. Choose an acid-free tape if that is important to you.

Fusible Web

Fusible web is a dry adhesive that needs heat from an iron to form a permanent bond between two surfaces. Brand names of fusible web include Wonder Under, Trans Web, and Steam-A-Seam. The Steam-A-Seam fusible web provides a temporary bond until heat is applied to form a permanent bond.

Fast2fuse Interfacing is a stiff interfacing with fusible web on both sides. It results in stiff pages that hold their shape well (Resources, page 110).

If you are interested in fusible web, buy a small quantity of each brand you find and experiment with the papers and fabrics you use to determine which one best suits your needs. Be sure to follow each manufacturer's instructions for the best results with their brand.

Gel Medium

Gel medium is an acrylic polymer that can be added to acrylic paints to extend their coverage. It also can be used as an adhesive. Gel mediums are available in a variety of weights and finishes from matte to gloss. Lightweight gel mediums are great for adhering paper and light fabric, whereas heavy gel medium is good for adhering heavier, bulkier items.

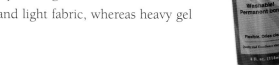

Glue Sticks

There are a vast number of fast-drying, easy-to-use glue sticks on the market. Many are available in either a permanent or temporary bond.

My favorite brand of glue stick is Uhu Stic, which is an acid-free product. This is the adhesive I take when traveling so that I can include things in my journal along the way, as well as the one I use in the studio when putting small and/or lightweight items in books.

Tip

Open an old catalog or outdated phone book to use as a base. You can spread glue or paint from the center past the edges for complete coverage. After removing your item from the page, simply turn to the next page. Instant clean work space!

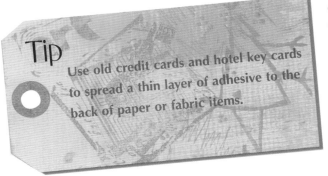

Tip

Use old credit cards and hotel key cards to spread a thin layer of adhesive to the back of paper or fabric items.

Spray Adhesives

There are many types of spray adhesives available. One thing they all have in common is that they must be used outside so you don't breathe the fumes: Trust me on this, no matter what the label says.

Spray adhesives are very convenient to use if you are in a hurry but may not be the best choice if you are concerned about the long-term effects of the chemicals in the adhesive.

Most spray adhesives are very strong, so make sure you place the item exactly where you want it. Repositioning is difficult, if not impossible.

Xyron adhesive system

Xyron

Xyron (pronounced Zy-ron) is the brand name of a line of products. Xyron machines apply a dry adhesive to the back of your item and require no electricity or batteries. Available in widths ranging from 5½" to 12", they can be found in most craft stores. Laminating cartridges, magnetic backings, acid-free, and adhesives that allow you to reposition items are also available.

The advantage of this system is that a dry adhesive won't distort your papers, and you don't have to wait for your adhesive to dry before continuing to work in your book. Xyron systems are pricey, so be sure you will use it enough to make the purchase worthwhile.

Still Stuck on Adhesives?

Refer to www.thistothat.com for more information on adhesives and their appropriate uses.

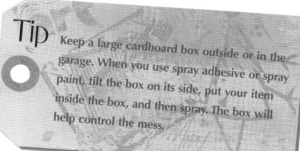

Tip Keep a large cardboard box outside or in the garage. When you use spray adhesive or spray paint, tilt the box on its side, put your item inside the box, and then spray. The box will help control the mess.

Batting

Batting is the middle layer in a quilt. Quilt batting is also an option for the middle layer in fabric book pages. You can buy batting made of wool, polyester, poly-cotton blends, silk, or cotton in a variety of weights. I like Quilters Dream Cotton batting, which comes in white or natural, is available in four different weights, and has no chemical binders.

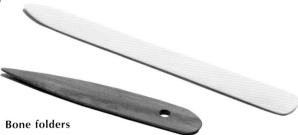

Bone Folder

A bone folder, used to create a sharp crease on paper, is traditionally made of bone (hence the name). You can also buy Teflon "bone" folders. Buy one that feels good in your hand.

Bone folders

Brayer

A brayer is a small roller used in printing to spread paint or ink thinly and evenly.

Brayers are made of different materials and are available in various sizes. They might be made of hard rubber, soft rubber, or foam. They come in widths from about 1½" to 8". (I think a 4" brayer is the most versatile size.)

You can also buy brayers with decorative elements molded into the rubber. Hearts, grid patterns, and stars are a few examples of the elements available on decorative brayers.

A variety of brayers

Brushes

Brushes can be used to apply paints, gesso, inks, adhesives, and watercolors to fabric and paper. Although there are very expensive brushes available, I prefer disposable foam brushes for most applications. I rinse them out right after I use them (if it's practical) and then throw them away when they get too stiff to be used.

Foam brush

Copyright

Copyright issues are important to consider in any medium. In simple terms, it is not acceptable to use images of other people's artwork and call it your own. I am not a legal expert, so the best I can do is point you in the right direction for learning about copyright issues. A terrific place to start is www.funnystrange.com/copyright/ when seeking information about copyright issues.

Craft Knife

A craft knife, sometimes referred to as an X-ACTO knife, can be used to cut paper, cardboard, plastic, and a variety of other materials. Always be careful when using this sharp tool and remember that a sharp blade is safer to use than a dull one.

Craft knives

Decorative-Edge Cutting Tools

Several companies make scissors and rotary cutter blades with different decorative patterns. Sharp rotary cutter blades that say they are intended for paper can often be used successfully on fabric, too.

Decorative-edge cutting tools

Ephemera

ephem·eron (i-'fe-mər-on)

Function: noun

1. something of no lasting significance—usually used in plural

2. ephemera plural: collectibles (as posters, broadsides, and tickets) not intended to have lasting value

—Merriam-Webster's Collegiate Dictionary, Tenth Edition copyright © 2002 by Merriam-Webster, Incorporated

Ephemera

According to collage artists, ephemera can be what makes an artwork unique. Each of us has different stuff in our lives, and using those scraps of memorabilia makes your artwork uniquely yours. Examples of ephemera include ticket stubs, shopping receipts, tags cut from clothing, stamps, handwritten notes, school report cards, invitations, candy wrappers, maps, travel brochures, and so forth.

Eyelets and Eyelet Setting Tools, Including Screw Punch

Eyelets come in myriad sizes, colors, and shapes. They are available at fabric, scrapbook, and craft stores. Proper tools are essential for the successful setting of eyelets. Choose tools appropriate for the size of the eyelets you are using. A ball-peen hammer is also convenient to keep in your studio.

Eyelets and setting tools

Hole punches include the manual, office-type hole punch; hole punches that you strike with a hammer to make the holes; and the Cadillac of hole punches, the Japanese screw punch shown here. Different-sized bits are also available. Although they aren't inexpensive, the screw punch and bits are well worth the investment if you will be punching lots of holes. If you suffer from carpal tunnel syndrome or other hand ailments, this tool will make your life easier.

Freezer Paper

Freezer paper, available at most grocery stores, is white paper with a plastic coating on one side. Intended for protecting food from freezer burn, its many great qualities have been discovered by quilters, who use it to work with fabric.

Place the freezer paper, shiny side down, onto the back of the fabric or fragile paper, then iron the matte side. The shiny coating creates a temporary bond with the fabric, which then can be run through your computer printer, folded and creased, or stitched to your book page. Peel away the freezer paper after using it if you want a softer feel. Leave it attached to your fabric for a sturdier product, such as for a fabric envelope.

Gesso

Gesso (pronounced "jesso") is an acrylic medium used to seal paper or fabric before painting. It prevents the paint from soaking through your paper or fabric and provides a "toothy" finish that accepts acrylic or oil mediums. Gesso is available in white or black, as well as a few other colors. Unless you plan to use a vast amount of a particular color, I recommend adding acrylic paint to white gesso to create your own colors.

Needles

Hand sewing needles are available in different sizes and tip styles. You will need a larger needle for yarn than for sewing thread, for example. The higher the number on the package, the larger the needle. If you don't already have hand sewing needles, buy a variety pack.

For best results, buy machine sewing needles made by the manufacturer of your sewing machine. You can purchase these from a retail dealer. Just as for hand sewing needles, the higher the number, the larger the needle. If you plan to stitch through multiple layers of fabric, paper, and/or batting, consider using a jeans needle, topstitching needle, or size 16 needle. When stitching through paper, a longer stitch length is best, to avoid tearing.

Tip

Most paper and fabric is made from plant fibers and can be treated similarly. When you are using your sewing machine to stitch on paper, however, you might notice that your needle gets dull quicker than when you are stitching fabric. Just remember to change your needle more often than you are used to, and your machine should behave itself!

Rotary Cutter, Ruler, and Self-Healing Mat

A rotary cutter looks like a pizza cutter—a very sharp, circular, cutting blade attached to a handle. They come in a variety of different blade sizes.

You need a special "self-healing" mat for rotary cutting. These mats are available in a variety of sizes to suit every need.

Acrylic rulers will help protect your fingers and hands while enabling you to make extremely straight and accurate cuts through multiple layers of fabric or paper.

Rotary cutting tools

Stamping Inks

Most stamping ink is available, ready to use, on an inkpad and as re-inkers, (bottles of the same color ink) to re-ink the pad. Re-inkers are great for use with brayers, stencils, and sponges on fabric and paper.

There are two basic types of stamping inks available: dye ink and pigment ink. Dye inks dry quicker than pigment inks. Pigment ink, because of its slower drying time, is easier to use when embossing your image. If you are not familiar with embossing, ask for a demonstration at a stamping store.

Tip The inside of junk mail envelopes often have wonderful patterned paper. Use them as they come, stamp on them, or add a wash of paint for color in your collage.

Pigment inks never dry on nonporous surfaces without help. Don't use pigment inks on glossy paper or vellum unless you heat set or emboss the image. To prevent smearing on porous (absorbent) surfaces, allow pigment inks to dry thoroughly before touching them.

Some inks are acid free; some are formulated for use on a wide variety of surfaces, including wood and metal; and some are more colorfast than others are. Read the packaging and ask questions at the store for more details on this quickly changing lineup of products.

Threads

Threads for machine and hand sewing are available in abundance. Polyester, cotton, silk, rayon, hand-dyed, metallic—you want it, chances are it is out there for you to find. In thread language, the lower the number, the thicker the thread. Keep this in mind when shopping. Look at quilt shops, needlework stores, and craft stores for interesting threads. Seek out a yarn shop if you are looking for novelty fibers to use in your next project.

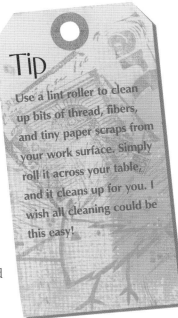

Tip Use a lint roller to clean up bits of thread, fibers, and tiny paper scraps from your work surface. Simply roll it across your table, and it cleans up for you. I wish all cleaning could be this easy!

Transparency Paper

Transparency paper is a see-through page that can be run through your computer printer or a copy machine. Depending on your image and whether you print in color or black and white, your image might be completely transparent or translucent. Transparencies are fun to use for layering images, making transfers, and adding variety to your work. Be sure to purchase sheets intended for use in your printer to prevent damage to your equipment.

Tools

Where to Find Supplies

Although you may already own many items you can use in your book projects, there always seems to be that one art supply or tool that you need and don't know where to find it. This section will help steer you in the right direction.

QUILT SHOP

Acrylic rulers

Beads

Buttons

Charms

Eyelet tape

Fabric: solids, themes, novelties, hand-dyes
—you name it, it's out there!

Fabric adhesive

Fabric pens

Fusible web

Hand and machine sewing needles and threads

Hooks and eyes

Premade bias tape

Quilt batting

Ribbon

Rotary cutters and blades

Self-healing cutting mat

Special fibers for hand and machine stitching

Specially prepared fabrics to run through your printer

Twill tape

Unique trims

Yarn

SCRAPBOOK STORE/ CRAFT STORE/RUBBER STAMP STORE

Acid-free paper

Bone folder

Decorative-edge cutting tools

Double-stick tape

Eyelets and eyelet setting tools

Liquid adhesive

Paper awl

Paper tags

Rubber stamps

Spray adhesive

Stamp pads and inks

Xyron machine

HARDWARE STORE

Foam brushes

Gloves to protect your hands from paint, gesso, and other materials

Masking tape

Metal fasteners

Metal ruler

OFFICE SUPPLY STORE

Acetate (transparencies)

Binder clips

Glue sticks

Labels

Page tabs

Paper shipping tags

Photo paper for your printer

Rings for binding pages together

FLEA MARKET

Buttons

Ephemera

Fabrics

Labels

Tags

Typewriters—to use or recycle parts

Vintage items

ART SUPPLY STORE

Acrylic paints

Bone folder

Brayer

Brushes for gesso and paint

X-ACTO knife

Fabric-printing inks

Gel medium

Gesso

ON A BUDGET?

Working on fabric and altered book projects doesn't have to drain your finances. There is plenty of stuff in your house (or that you can find for free) that makes wonderful art material. This list is just the tip of the iceberg—once you start collecting cool items to use in your books, you'll have a new eye for appreciating the potential of everything you see.

Bits of things collected on walks

Button collection

Buttons recycled off worn-out or outgrown garments

Claim checks

Clothing tags cut from garments

Coasters from restaurants

Coffee grounds and tea bags (to color paper and fabric)

Corrugated cardboard from boxes, light bulb packaging, or "cozy sleeves" from the coffee shop

Cotton balls and swabs (to apply paint, chalk, or glue, as well as to clean up excess)

Discontinued wallpaper sample books—often free for the asking as new patterns are introduced

Egg cartons to sort beads, buttons, and eyelets, as well as to mix small amounts of paint

Envelopes—used or new

Expired licenses from fishing, hunting, or pet tags

Eye shadow as "chalk" on paper or fabric— just be sure to seal it so it doesn't rub off

Fingernail polish in colors you don't use anymore (to color paper or even write text on fabric)

Foil from candy wrappers and gum

Game and puzzle pieces from incomplete or outgrown games and puzzles

Glue

Heavyweight glassine paper used to package breakfast cereals, which can be used to protect your work surface from paint or glue, as a release paper—like wax paper, or crumpled to create texture, painted, and then punched out to create unique embellishments

Keys

Kids' homework

Leftover bits of wallpaper

Maps

Netting from produce sacks to paint and stamp a background pattern or painted and incorporated onto your page

Old watch parts from broken watches

Paper brads

Photos—photocopy them to keep the originals intact

Plastic cards (such as expired credit cards) to spread glue or paint

Receipts

Recycled greeting cards and old calendars for collages in your books

Sand mixed with paint to create texture

Seed pods

Shoe bottoms painted to create an interesting pattern when stamped on fabric or paper

Sponges—unused cosmetic sponges, car washing sponges, or kitchen sponges

Styrofoam trays from the deli for disposable palettes for glue or paint

Tags from the dry cleaners or auto repair shop

Tyvek envelopes

Upholstery-fabric sample books—often free for the asking as new fabrics are introduced

Used postage stamps and postmarks

Used dryer sheets glued onto the page and painted over for texture

Used file folders—to cut up, to paint, to make tags, or to cut stencils

Vegetables used to stamp images

Wax paper

Wallpaper paste to make original paste paper

Wildflowers pounded onto fabric to create subtle background color

Window screening

Wine bottle corks to create your own stamps

Wrapping paper and ribbon

Don't Sew? And Don't Want To?

If you don't sew and don't even want to try, don't count yourself out when it comes to including fabric in your books. There are many alternatives to machine or hand sewing embellishments into altered books and scrapbooks. Try using button stickers, or glue buttons instead of sewing them onto your page. Buy prestitched envelopes and paper pockets from the scrapbook store. Use self-adhesive zippers and sticky rickrack on paper and fabric book projects. Use fabric glue to secure items together instead of stitching them. Fuse layers of fabrics together with fusible web instead of stitching them together.

Find a rubber stamp with marks that could substitute for stitches. Stamp it on paper and fabric to simulate hand stitching. Use a fabric marker to draw stitches onto your fabric instead of using thread. Iron-on threads and ribbons also are available for your projects. Use scrapbook paper with stitching lines already on it. If you want to try real stitching but don't have much money to invest in a sewing machine, look at a craft store (or thrift store) for an inexpensive machine. You'll learn whether you like the look of stitches enough to save up for a "real" machine in the future.

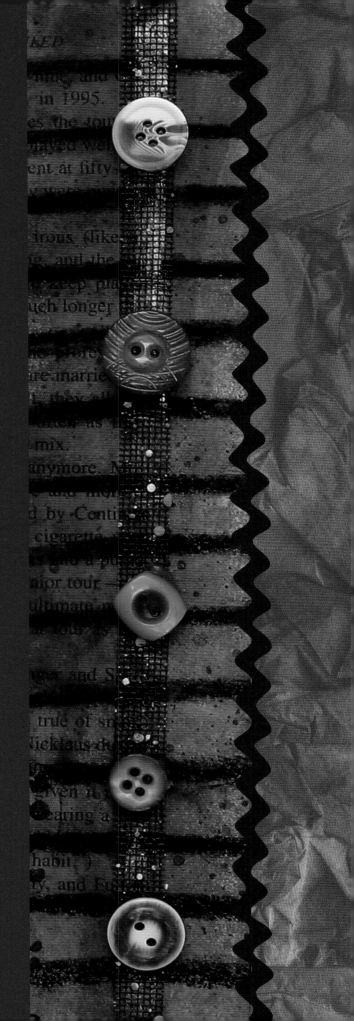

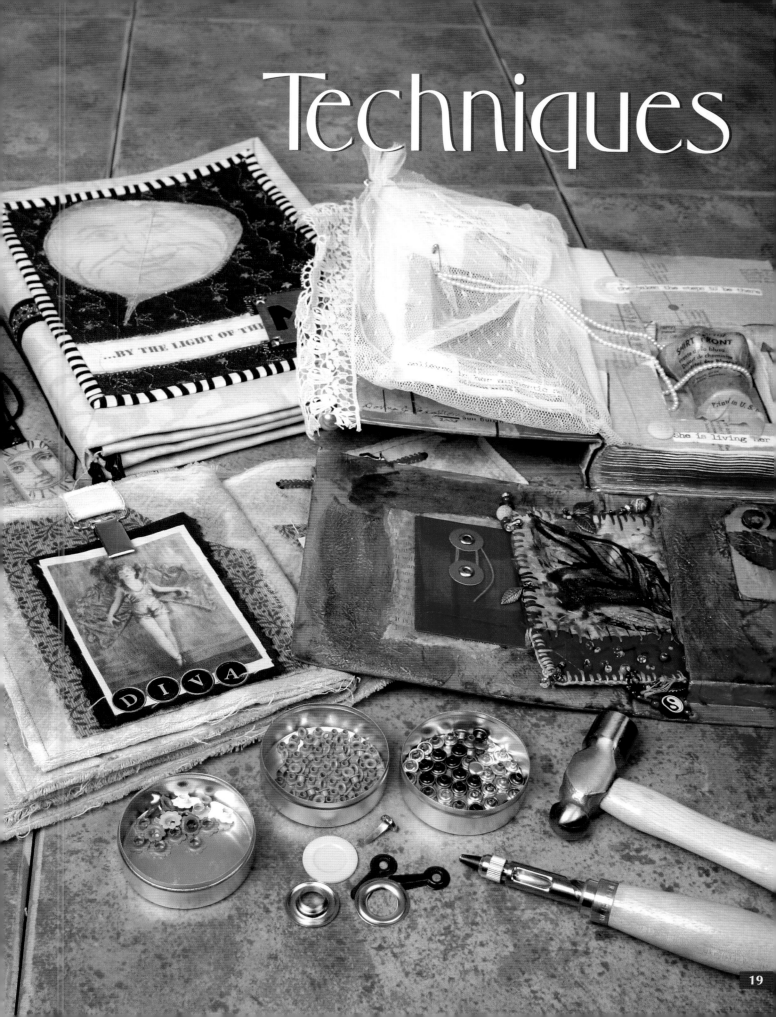

Techniques

Setting Eyelets

eyelets can be functional or purely decorative. They can attach items to your page, hold pages together, or lend a bit of color and provide a touch of whimsy to your pages. There are several different sizes of eyelets; they also are available in myriad colors, shapes, and finishes.

Tip Clean, used acrylic cutting boards make a wonderful surface for punching holes and hammering eyelets. These are especially useful if you work on your dining room table. You certainly don't want to punch into the wood accidentally!

HOW TO SET AN EYELET

Be sure you have an appropriately-sized hole punch to punch the right hole for your eyelet. You might use a manual single-hole punch; a "hit-with-a-hammer" hole punch; or a Japanese screw punch. See the Tools, Supplies, Terminology & Tips section (page 9) and Resources (page 110) for more information about these tools. Practice makes perfect.

1 Punch the hole through all the layers you want to join with the eyelet.

2 Place the eyelet in the hole.

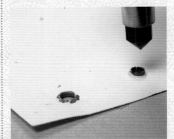

3 Turn the eyelet and fabric (or paper) right side up and place it on a firm surface. Take your eyelet-setting tool and a hammer, and firmly tap the hammer onto the tool two or three times. Check to see if the edges have started flaring out. It is the flaring out of the back of the eyelet that holds the layers of paper and/or fabric together.

4 I like to finish the process by lightly tapping the back of the eyelet with the rounded end of a ball-peen hammer to help smooth the backside of the eyelet.

Pattern Tissue Uses

d ressmaker's tissue, pattern tissue, tissue paper . . . whatever you call it, it is incredibly versatile paper. It can be made into wonderful handmade paper, serve as translucent template material, or be crumpled and dyed or painted and then smoothed out to make beautiful textured backgrounds. .

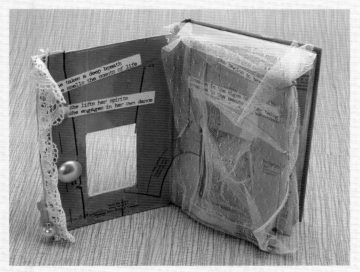

Donna J. Engstrom used pattern tissue as a background for her daughter's original poetry in She.

Pattern tissue is the base on the cover of Donna J. Engstrom's altered book She.

Joyce M.A. Gary used a collage of pattern tissue as a background in Juxtaposition.

Diana L. Klimt-Perenick sandwiched dried flowers between layers of pattern tissue in A Common Thread.

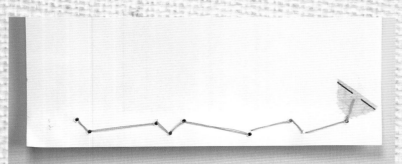

Instead of knots, pattern tissue was glued to secure thread ends to the back of a page.

Carol Owen used pattern tissue enhanced with thin acrylic paints on the cover of her altered book Bingo.

Chapter 5

MATE
ONS

*Pattern tissue glued to the edge of a block
of pages can hold them together.*

*Using pattern tissue was appropriate on my
"Grandma Taught Me To Sew" page in* How I Got Here.

Fabric Frames

a fabric frame can be used to enhance photographs, draw attention to an element in your collage, or as a subtle accent on your page layout.

THE SIMPLEST FRAME

This simple frame is made with a single background fabric placed underneath your image. Glue or stitch your fabric (by hand or machine) onto your book page.

A simple, hand-stitched frame by Diana L. Klimt-Perenick in A Common Thread. *The image was a free download from www.scraps-n-more.com.*

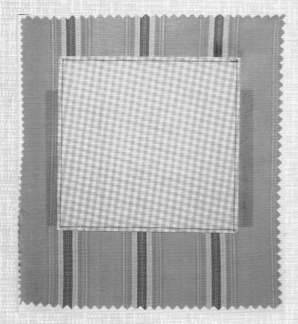

1 Apply your photograph, transfer, or collage onto a piece of fabric and trim to size.

2 Cut a larger piece of fabric and place it behind the first fabric to make the frame.

3 Stitch or glue the two fabrics together.

4 Apply fusible web or glue to the wrong side of the back fabric and adhere it onto your book page.

A simple frame hand stitched by Kerrie E. Carbary in her altered book Field Book of Common Rocks and Minerals

A simple frame with hand stitching and paint highlights

SOFT-EDGE FRAME

This simple frame is enhanced by the soft edges that result from tearing fabric or using a decorative-edge rotary blade.

1 Make a collage, choose a photograph, or make a transfer onto a piece of fabric.

2 Cut the fabric edges with a decorative-edge rotary cutter or tear 4 strips of another fabric to fit around your central image.

3 Glue or use fusible web to adhere your image onto your page.

4 Glue or use fusible web to adhere the fabric frame strips around your central image.

Torn-edge frame by Kristin Steiner in
My Blue Book of Longing

SUEDE OR LEATHER STAMPED FRAME

Leather and suede take paint beautifully. I love the texture and nap that some suede offers. When stamping, choose a simple stamp that will look good even if your image doesn't stamp perfectly. It is a good idea to heat set the paint or ink so it doesn't rub off or transfer onto another surface. Follow the manufacturer's instructions included with your product for heat-setting information.

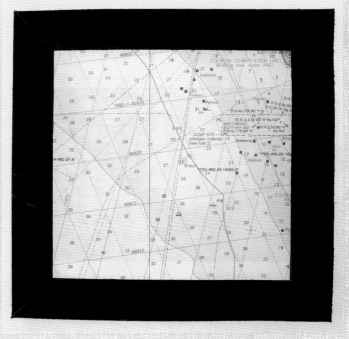

1 Cut your central image slightly smaller than the size of your page.

2 Cut 4 strips of leather or suede to fit your central image.

3 Use the 45° markings on your clear ruler to miter the corners of your leather strips.

4 Stamp the leather strips.

5 Attach your central image onto your book page.

6 Carefully glue and place your leather strips in place, adjusting as necessary to fit.

7 Place a layer of wax paper over your finished page and set weights on it while it dries.

Note: Thrift stores can be wonderful sources for leather and suede garments. These affordable, used garments can be cut up and incorporated into your next art project.

LOG CABIN FRAME

This frame is based on the traditional Log Cabin quilting block. The center square or rectangle is surrounded by contrasting pieces of fabric, or "logs." The logs for this frame are cut asymmetrically, but you can cut them symmetrically if you prefer.

1 Cut one strip from each of four fabrics.

2 Machine sew a strip to the right-hand side of your image.

3 Press, being careful not to harm your photograph. Note: If you have a photograph on paper, use a pressing cloth to help protect the photograph from the heat of your iron.

4 Sew a strip to the bottom of your photograph.

5 Press carefully.

6 Repeat for the two remaining sides.

7 Apply premade fusible bias tape to cover the raw edges of your fabric strips.

8 Use spray adhesive or a thin layer of glue and position your framed photo on your page.

Log Cabin frame with torn edges and hand stitching in Kristin Steiner's My Blue Book of Longing

PRINTED TWILL FRAME

Many companies now offer printed twill tape for scrapbooks, altered books, and other embellishment options. These are terrific products, but you might want to create some original printed twill with your choice of words on it. Twill tape comes in a variety of widths and can be painted or dyed to your desired color before printing.

Custom Printing on Twill Tape

Note: Some printers may not cooperate with this technique. Test carefully to make sure this technique will work for you.

1 Determine the line length and font size that will fit the twill tape and print your desired text onto plain printer paper, double or triple spacing the text to leave plenty of room between the lines.

2 Carefully cover each line of text with double-stick tape.

3 Position your twill tape on top of the double-stick tape, trimming the ends and making sure that the tape does not extend beyond the width of your printer paper.

4 Rub the twill tape firmly with your fingers to attach it thoroughly to the tape.

5 Run the paper back through your printer. Because you taped directly over the text, the printer should print right on the twill tape.

Making the Printed Twill Frame

Choose your background fabric and cut or tear it slightly smaller than your finished page.

1 Machine stitch, hand stitch, or glue the twill tape onto your background fabric.

2 Glue your background fabric onto your page.

3 Finish your collage by adding central elements, a pocket or envelope, a photograph, an embellished tag, some favorite buttons, or just use the printed twill to frame a novelty fabric.

Carol Owen used commercially printed twill tape to frame this vintage photograph in her book Bingo.

Retro frame with eyelets and cording

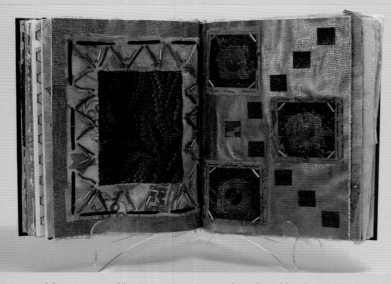

Layered frames created by Joyce M.A. Gary in her altered book Juxtaposition. *She combines beads, buttons, cheesecloth, hand-dyed fabric, and hand stitching in this wonderful spread.*

LAYERED FRAME

Layer coordinating fabrics in various sizes and let them create their own frames. Look for fabrics that speak to you when you visit your local quilt shop—the themes available are practically endless!

1 Cut out your central image.

2 Layer and fuse or stitch it to a second, slightly larger fabric.

3 Tear or cut a third, even larger fabric.

4 Fuse or sew the top two fabrics to the third.

5 Repeat as needed to create your desired effect.

6 Glue onto your page.

7 Add eyelet embellishments, buttons, or beads to accent your image.

Note: After I threaded the wire through the eyelets and bent the ends around to the back of the page, I applied some glue to the wire tails to hold them in place. Then I glued this page to the following page for stability and to ensure that the wire didn't poke through the paper.

INSPIRATION FOR YOUR NEXT FRAME-UP

Here are some more great samples to inspire you.

Lelainia N. Lloyd created a double frame on the cover of 3 Ring Circus. The row of buttons acts as the first frame, and the wide black rickrack frames the entire cover.

Don't limit yourself to only framing one image on your page. Consider framing the entire spread, as Lelainia did on this page in her fabric book Every Family Has One.

Lelainia creates a wonderful frame with ribbon in her Every Family Has One *fabric book.*

This simple frame was created by stamping the same image twice: once directly on the page, and once on vellum.

Stamp by Just For Fun.

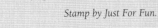

Kristin Steiner machine stitched narrow wavy fabric strips to frame her Colorado landscape in My Blue Book of Longing.

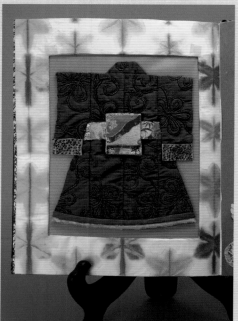

Delores Hamilton created frames covered in Japanese paper on each page of her book Ceremonial Kimonos.

Julia Slebos created this effective frame in 19th Century Babes by removing paper from in front of the image. This idea would be fun in fabric, too.

Stamp by Magenta

Martine House gives inspiration to everyone who likes to embroider with the exquisite details in her Legacy book.

Section Edges

Note: In most cases, you will want to have completed the artwork on your pages before you finish the edges.

When you are working in an altered book, you often want to group a section of pages together to support the weight of the embellishments or reduce the number of decorated pages needed to complete the book. By creating a section of pages, you control how many pages of your book will become artwork and how many provide a supporting role.

This section contains instructions and illustrations for a few methods to finish the edges of those pages. Your goal should not be to copy exactly any of these ideas in your next project. Instead, your challenge is to use these ideas, mixing and matching them, add your own imprint, and create a piece that is uniquely your own.

Note: If you work on single sheets of paper in a more traditional scrapbook format, these techniques are easily accomplished on one or more edges of your scrapbook page layouts for extra interest and texture.

Hand sewing the ribbon edge:

1 Punch holes and thread your ribbon or yarn through the holes.

2 Attach beads or buttons to the ends of the ribbon.

3 Tie a knot and add a dab of glue or fray stop to the tips of the ribbon to prevent raveling.

Eyelet ribbon edge:

1 Punch holes and attach your eyelets through all the layers.

2 Thread the ribbon or yarn through the eyelets.

3 Add beads, buttons, or knots to the ends of the ribbon.

Juliana Coles hand stitched the edge of her journal page with sewing thread.

Pattern tissue edge:

1 Cut or tear a strip of pattern tissue approximately the same height as your book pages. Use a piece a little more than twice as wide as your desired finished width, so that it wraps around to the backside plus the thickness of your section.

2 Rub gel medium onto the back of the tissue paper.

3 Lay the pattern tissue on the front page of your section.

4 Wrap the tissue paper around the edge of the pages to the back of the section.

5 If there is any excess tissue at the top or bottom, fold the excess over the section.

6 Press firmly all over the tissue to ensure it is in contact with the entire section surface.

7 Wrap wax paper loosely around the tissue paper, close the book with the wax paper inside, put some weight on top, and let it dry.

Note: If you don't have any gel medium, you might experiment with white glue. Always test a product before using it in a project.

Eyelet and leather edge:

1 Cut a piece of eyelet tape the same height as your pages.

2 Lay it on top of the first page in your section.

3 Use a pencil to mark a dot onto the page through the center of each eyelet.

4 Remove the eyelet tape from your book.

5 Punch through all layers of paper at each mark.

6 Place the eyelet tape back on page.

7 Cut 4" strips of leather, insert, and tie one through each eyelet.

Note: You could use yarn, ribbon, or cotton cord in place of the leather strips. You also might want to put a dot of glue on the back of the eyelet tape between the eyelets, especially at the upper and lower edges.

Button edge:

1 Punch holes.

2 Stitch through the holes with thread, yarn, or ribbon. Go through each hole as many times as you want, to achieve the look you desire.

3 At the last hole at the top and bottom (or wherever you prefer), add buttons or beads.

Happy Hair

139

Rickrack edge:

1 Cut rickrack to the length you want. It can be exactly the same height as your pages, shorter than your pages, or long enough that it hangs over the top and bottom edges of your pages.

2 With a small amount of adhesive, glue the rickrack to your page.

3 Punch holes through the rickrack and the paper at the same time.

4 Stitch through the rickrack and paper, attaching beads (or buttons) in a few places.

Bead-dangle edge:

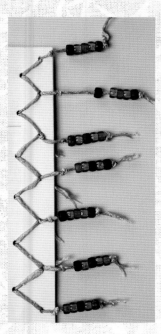

1 Punch holes approximately 1" apart in a zigzag pattern through all the pages at the same time.

2 Use yarn, ribbon, or heavy embroidery thread to stitch the pages together.

3 Add beads at every hole, every other hole, or only the top hole.

Wide rickrack edge:

1 Cut a piece of wide rickrack a little longer than the height of your page.

2 Apply glue on the back of the rickrack.

3 Place the rickrack onto the page in the book, lining up the edge of the page with the approximate center of the rickrack.

4 Wrap the rickrack around to the back of the section.

5 Place under a weight until dry. Sew through the rickrack and pages to attach buttons or beads if desired.

Note: You also could hand sew the rickrack to the pages, or machine stitch it if you are able to get the page edges close enough to your sewing machine needle.

Sheer-ribbon button edge:

1 Cut the ribbon to your desired length. This technique looks great when the ribbon extends beyond the edges of your page.

2 Arrange buttons over the ribbon. Sew through the buttons and pages to secure the pages, ribbon, and buttons together.

Note: You could use twill tape or a strip of fabric instead of sheer ribbon.

Fabric and ribbon edge:

1 Cut 2 strips of fabric a little longer than the height of the book. I used a wavy-edge rotary blade.

2 Decide how you want to overlap your fabrics.

3 Spray adhesive onto the back of your fabric. Place it onto your page and wrap around the edges to the back of your section of pages. Punch holes along the edges, through all the layers of fabric and paper.

4 Thread ribbon or yarn through the holes.

5 Glue the tail of the ribbon to the backside of the pages.

Sutured fabric edge:

1 Cut a piece of gauze (or other fabric) long enough to wrap around the edge of the paper.

2 Cut or tear a piece of fabric to fit the rest of the page.

3 Glue or otherwise adhere your fabric to your book page.

4 Wrap the gauze around the section edge and hold it in place. Use a small amount of glue or double-stick tape on the backside of the gauze to anchor the the fabric to the back of the section.

5 Sew on buckles, beads, or elastic bandage fasteners making sure to catch both fabrics in your stitching.

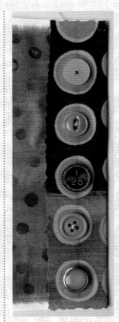

Button edge:

1 Use fusible web or other adhesive to attach your background fabric onto your page.

2 Cut a strip of accent fabric the same height as your page. For the width, double the desired finished width of the edge strip, and add enough fabric to wrap around pages.

3 Use fabric glue or fusible web to adhere an accent fabric onto your section, wrapping it around to the backside.

4 Attach buttons, game pieces, beads, or found objects to your fabric.

Julia Slebos successfully combines wire, twig, raffia, yarn, and embroidery thread on the edges of this collage spread in 19th Century Babes.

Finished Fabric Edges

I love the soft edge that results from tearing fabrics. Some fabrics don't tear as well as others, so you might find yourself looking for other options to finish the edges of your fabric pages. If you are using a lightweight fabric, your page might benefit from the addition of quilt batting or heavyweight interfacing (like fast2fuse, page 10 and 111). Let's explore some alternative edge treatments.

Note: In most cases, you will want to have completed the artwork on your pages before finishing the fabric edges.

MAKING A TORN FABRIC PAGE

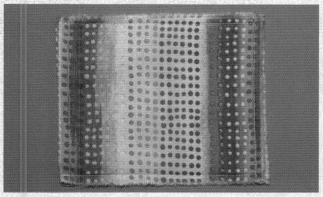

With the fabric wrong sides together, machine or hand sew around the perimeter of the page. Leave the soft, torn edges exposed.

MAKING A PILLOWCASE FABRIC PAGE

1 Cut 2 pieces of fabric the size of a book page plus ¼" seam allowances.

2 With the fabric right sides together, sew around the fabric page with a ¼" seam allowance.

3 Trim the corners at a 45° angle to reduce the bulk of fabric. Be careful not to trim too close or cut the stitches.

4 Turn the fabric page right side out, like you would a pillowcase. Smooth the seams, encourage the corners to cooperate, and press if necessary.

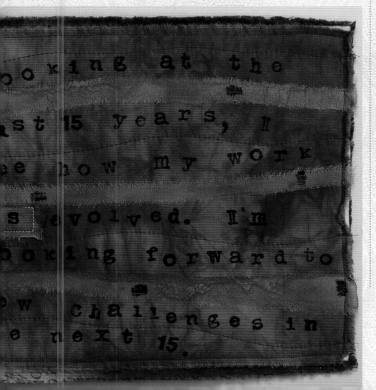

Techniques

QUILT BINDING EDGE

If you are a quiltmaker, you are very familiar with quilt bindings. We can use that traditional finish to complete fabric book pages too!

1 Cut a strip of fabric for binding. For these samples, the binding strip was cut 1¾" wide. On small pages, a narrow binding will look great. The larger the page, the wider the binding should be.

2 Press the binding in half lengthwise, wrong sides together.

3 Starting on one edge, match the raw edges of your binding strip with the raw edge of your fabric page.

4 Sew through all layers using a ¼" seam allowance. Stop ¼" from the edge and stitch diagonally to the corner of your page.

5 Carefully remove the page from your sewing machine and fold the binding strip backward so that the edge of the binding strip is in line with the edge of your fabric page.

 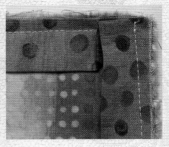

6 Fold the binding strip back down over the page, being careful to line up the edge of the fold with the edge of your fabric page.

7 Starting at the top edge of the binding strip, back stitch and sew through all layers to within ¼" of the next corner.

 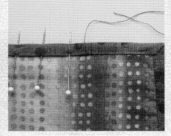

8 Repeat Steps 4–7 to sew the binding onto as many sides of your page as you desire.

9 Fold the binding strip around the edge of your fabric page to the other side.

10 Pin the folded edge in place, ensuring that it covers your stitching line.

11 Hand sew, using a blind stitch, to secure the binding to the fabric page.

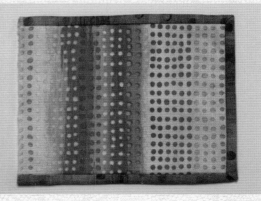

12 Continue around the page until all edges are complete. The raw-edge side will be attached in the final book binding.

TWILL TAPE EDGE FINISH

Twill tape or wide ribbon also can be used to finish the edge of your fabric book pages. This technique is a little quicker than quilt bindings because there are no raw edges on the twill or ribbon. If you can't find the color twill tape you want, just paint or dye it before applying it to your book page.

Note: Glue is also a possibility if you don't want to sew, but you will have to hold the twill or ribbon in place while the glue sets.

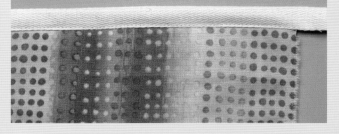

5 Machine or hand stitch through all layers.

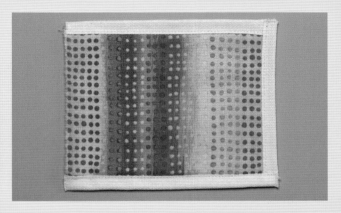

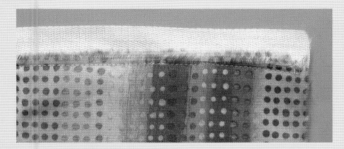

1 Cut your twill or ribbon to the same measurements as your page.

2 Lay the twill lengthwise underneath the edge of the page, overlapping the edge a little less than halfway across the width of the twill.

3 Machine or hand stitch through all layers, using about a ¼" seam allowance.

4 Wrap the rest of the twill around the page and pin in place.

6 Repeat Steps 1–5 for all sides of your pages. The raw-edge side will be attached in the final book binding.

On By the Light of the Moon, *Julia Slebos used a fabric binding on the edge of the pages.*

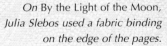

HAND-STITCHED EDGE FINISH

You also can hand sew around the edges of your fabric to finish your pages. Depending on your sewing style and the thread you use, you might create a primitive look or a refined edge. I like to use embroidery floss, perle cotton thread, thick hand-dyed thread, ribbon floss, or even yarn to hand stitch page edges.

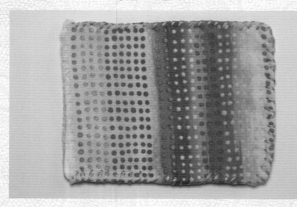

Hand stitch around the edges, pulling the thread taut enough to "round over" the raw edges of your fabric and create a nice rolled edge. I prefer the look of less-than-perfect stitching, so don't worry if your stitch size varies. Enjoy the charm of your personal stitches.

Tip

Want to hand stitch evenly and don't think you can? Use the holes from the edges of computer paper or Tiger tape as your "template" to even out your stitches.

Carol Vasenko hand stitched charming edges on her Yellow Ladder quiltlet inside this wonderful journal box.

For Unleaving, Carol Vasenko combines an array of colors and stitch lengths to attach the hand-carved stamp image and finish the edges of her quiltlet.

Andrea Stern uses embroidery floss to finish the edges of her fabric book cover for A Hunk, A Duck. Notice the hand stitching on the other layers of fabric on the cover.

here may be a time when you want to include lots of information in your altered book or on your scrapbook page. Perhaps you'd like to do some personal journaling, but you don't want everyone who sees your work to be able to read everything. Maybe you've been on a fabulous trip and have lots of brochures, ticket stubs, maps, and memorabilia that you want to save but don't know how to keep everything together. Pockets and envelopes can be an ideal solution in these situations. They offer visual interest to your book page while providing you with extra storage space.

POCKETS FROM GARMENTS

An easy way to get a pocket onto your book or scrapbook page is to use an already-sewn pocket from a garment, such as an old flannel shirt pocket or the pocket from an outgrown pair of favorite jeans. Or consider recycling a yard-sale find by incorporating its pockets into your next project.

VARIATIONS: You might glue the pocket into your book and hand stitch around the edges. Or you could use a band of buttons around the outside edge, especially if you use a dress shirt. This would be a great time to use some of those miscellaneous buttons that seem to multiply in your button box. Use the pocket to hold a decorated tag, a favorite photograph, a travel brochure, a map, or a handwritten letter from someone special.

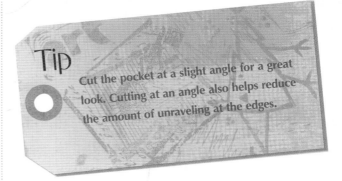

Tip

Cut the pocket at a slight angle for a great look. Cutting at an angle also helps reduce the amount of unraveling at the edges.

SHEER FABRIC POCKET

I love the look of sheer fabrics in books. They allow you a glimpse of what's inside, providing intrigue. You can use sheer silk, organza, vellum paper, or recycle the fabric from a sheer blouse to provide an interesting texture to your next page.

OPTIONAL: Finish the edge that will be the top of the pocket. This adds strength if you use the pocket for holding items.

Tip When putting eyelets into thin fabrics or fragile papers, consider using eyelet washers between the eyelet and the fabric or paper. These help reinforce the fragile fibers and add to their durability in your finished piece.

Cut the pocket from the garment, including some surrounding fabric. Apply glue or fusible web to the back of the pocket and attach it. Add eyelets, buttons, or beads.

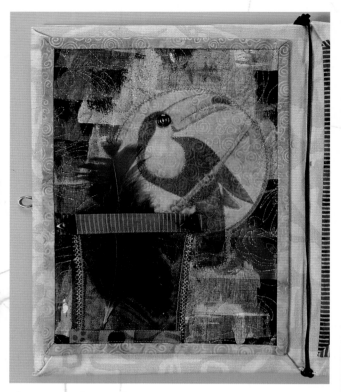

This amazing sheer pocket is in Julia Slebos's fabric book By the Light of the Moon. *In addition to the great button-accented pocket that holds feathers, this quiltlet includes organza, hand-painted fabric, and machine quilting.*

Image: Teesha Moore collage clip sheet

1 Cut or tear hand-dyed fabric for the background.

2 Apply fusible web to the back, leaving the protective paper on for now.

3 Cut a sheer fabric to make a pocket the size you prefer.

4 Placing the sheer fabric on the background, attach eyelets and thread with ribbon or yarn, if desired. If you use buttons or beads, space them closely enough that items won't fall out of the pocket. Consider gluing some of the sheer fabric to the facing page to tie the two pages together visually.

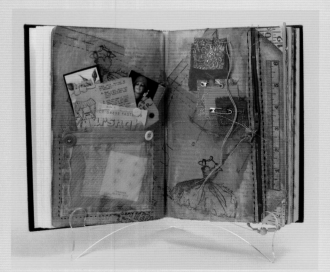

Julia Slebos incorporated this gorgeous sheer pocket into her altered book Sew It Seems. *The images seen through the sheer fabric are so enticing! Notice the great zipper accent on the facing page.*

Kristin Steiner created this clear pocket by machine stitching part of a page protector onto a fabric page in My Blue Book of Longing.

BUTTON POCKET

Use a selection of monochromatic buttons for a serene look, mix bright colors and a variety of sizes and shapes to attract lots of attention, or pay homage to an earlier time by including vintage buttons when accenting your pocket page.

1 Cut or tear a piece of fabric to the size of your page.

2 Glue or stitch this piece of fabric to a right-hand (background) page.

3 Cut or tear a second piece of fabric that is the same width as your page but twice the height + 4".

4 Glue or stitch this second piece of fabric to the back of the page preceding the background page, and wrap it around to also cover the front of the page.

5 If you used glue, place wax paper between the pages, close the book, and place it under some weights to dry.

6 Fold the wrapped page down at a 45° angle to create the pocket.

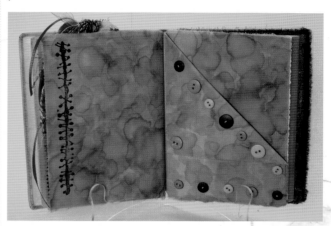

7 Add buttons or beads along the folded edge of the pocket, stitching through just the top page.

8 Add buttons, beads, or stitching along the bottom edge and the side of the pocket to hold the layers together.

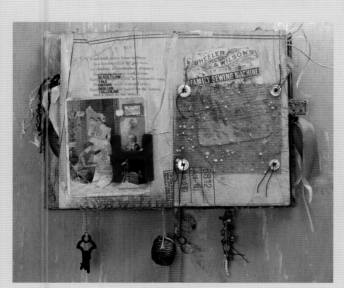

Carol Owen very effectively uses mesh fabric to create a pocket in her Bingo altered book. Notice the wonderful warmth created by the pattern tissue background.

Lenna Andrews Foster successfully incorporates a mesh pocket for photographs in her accordion fabric book My Mother—Myself. Notice the wonderful typewriter alphabet stickers used to title the page.

STITCHED POCKET

If you like to do hand stitching, here is a terrific, quick project. If you choose fabric and thread colors that you are comfortable working with, you'll be amazed at how many of your other fabrics and papers coordinate with your completed pocket.

Carol Owen machine stitched these layers of paper together to create a pocket in her altered book *Bingo*. Most techniques for fabric can be used successfully with paper or a combination of fabric and paper.

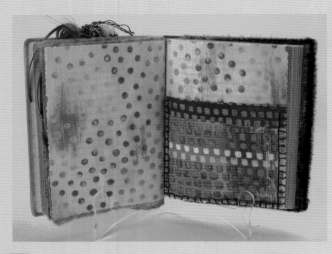

1 Cut or tear a piece of fabric for the page background.

2 Cut a piece of pocket fabric the width of your page. The height of the piece should equal the finished height of your pocket plus enough fabric to turn over to form a flap along the top edge.

3 Hand stitch, topstitch, or glue the flap of the pocket along the top edge of the pocket.

4 Attach the pocket to the background with decorative hand or machine stitches.

5 Glue the background and pocket into your book.

6 Place wax paper between the pages, close the book, and place it under some weights to dry.

Here's another great pocket from Carol Owen's Bingo *book. Pockets don't always have to open at the top. This one opens to the side of the book and has wonderful, hand-stitched accents. Notice the machine stitching on top of the collaged paper tag.*

Don't limit yourself to squares and rectangles when you think about pockets. Look at the lovely curves Martine House created on one of the pockets in her constructed fabric book Legacy.

LIBRARY CHECK-OUT CARD POCKET

Although many library checkout systems are now computerized, I still love the traditional library check-out card book pockets.

Note: Although you can use glue to put these layers together, I like the extra crispness that results from using fusible web for those pockets.

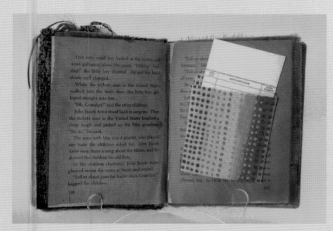

1 Cut a sheer piece of fabric to fit your book page.

2 Coat your page with glue and smooth the sheer fabric onto it (it doesn't need to be perfectly flat).

3 Use a copy machine to reduce or enlarge the check-out library card book pocket template pattern (page 50) to fit your needs. Cut out the template.

4 Fuse 2 pieces of fabric, larger than the template pattern, wrong sides together, with fusible web. You can choose 2 contrasting fabrics or the same fabric on both sides of your pocket. Both sides will show on your finished pocket.

5 Trace around the template pattern and cut out your fabric envelope.

6 Fold and glue the sides and bottom of the pocket, following the folding order on the template.

7 Place wax paper around the pocket and set weights on it to dry.

8 Using heavy-duty adhesive, glue the pocket to the book page.

9 Place wax paper between the pages, close the book, and place it under some weights to dry.

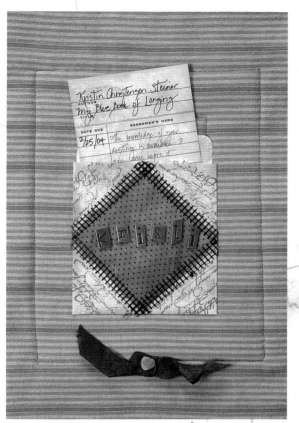

In My Blue Book of Longing, *Kristin Steiner used fabric to embellish a paper library check-out card book pocket that includes a library card containing a quote.*

SLANTED POCKET

This yields a lot of space for photos and ephemera.

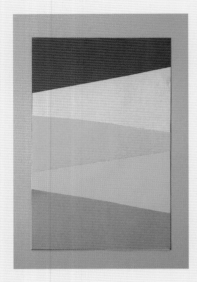

1 Measure your book page. This will be the maximum size of your first and largest template.

2 Make your largest template.

3 Make 5 paper templates—the largest one the size of the book page and the rest progressively smaller—slanted on the top edge. (They could be straight across the top if you prefer.)

4 Choose the number of fabrics you want to use for your pockets.

5 Cut out the largest piece of fabric.

6 Cut out the second-largest pocket.

7 Lay it on top of the background piece.

8 Place your photograph or other item between the layers of fabric and draw a line just below the lowest point you want the photo to reach.

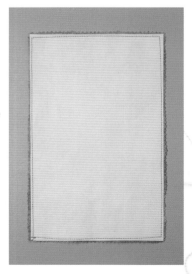

Optional: Stitch it to a piece of paper, which will be the base that you glue into your book.

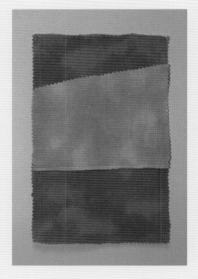

9 Sew on that line.

Note: If you don't do this, photos and other items can drop all the way to the bottom of your page and be difficult to reach.

10 Trim the excess fabric below the seam line to eliminate bulk and avoid wasting fabric.

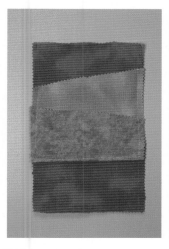

OPTIONS/VARIATIONS:
Sew rickrack, soutache braid, twill tape (stamped, printed, or plain), quilt binding, seam tape, rows of beads, buttons, fusible bias tape, lace, or other ornamentation across the top of each pocket piece before stitching it down. Or fold the fabric over so there are no raw edges across the top of the pockets.

11 Cut out the third-largest pocket.

12 Lay it on top of the previous two.

13 Repeat Steps 7–11 to add the remaining pockets. The smallest pockets probably won't have any excess to trim away.

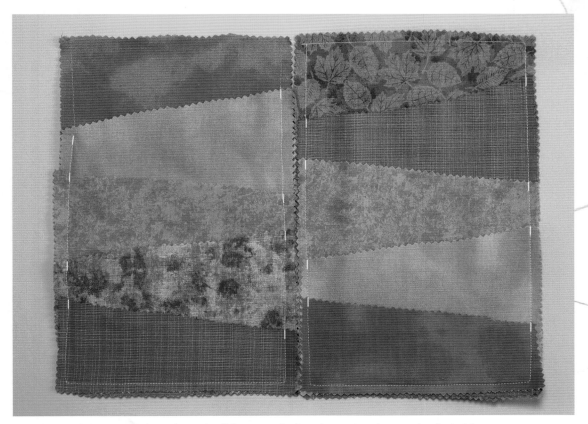

Stitch around the outer edges, through all layers including the optional paper, backstitching a few stitches at the outside edges of each pocket for additional strength. If you are making a pocket page for the facing page, repeat Steps 5–11. You can reverse the templates to mirror the angles and switched the location of the fabrics for variety.

FABRIC ENVELOPES

Envelopes are a terrific visual element. They pique our curiosity about what might be inside and add a touch of dimension to an otherwise flat layout. If you would like to include something private on your page, an envelope might be a great way to keep it hidden from others.

Note: Although you can use glue to put the layers together, I like the extra crispness that results from using fusible web for envelopes.

1 Fuse 2 different fabrics, wrong sides together, with fusible web.

2 Use a copy machine to reduce or enlarge the envelope template pattern (page 49). Cut out your template.

3 Trace around the template and cut out your fabric envelope.

4 Punch holes around the outside edges of the envelope. *Note: If you prefer to machine stitch, skip this step and use one of the decorative stitches on your sewing machine to finish the edge of your envelope.*

5 Hand or machine stitch around the edge. I added some nonfunctional eyelets with Ultrasuede circles as accents. You could make these decorative circles functional by paying attention to their placement and adding a string to keep the envelope closed.

6 Fold and glue the sides and bottom of the envelope, following the folding order on the template.

7 Use heavy-duty adhesive on the back of the envelope, being careful to keep the flap free of adhesive.
Tip: You can place some masking tape across the flap of the envelope to keep the adhesive from spreading.

8 Place wax paper between the pages, close the book, and place it under some weights to dry.

Fabric: Lonni Rossi, Typospheres Collection (outside of envelope); Nancy Crow for Kent Avery (inside of envelope)

In My Blue Book of Longing, Kristin Steiner added this vintage paper envelope to her fabric page. Notice the addition of a special button to wrap string around to secure the closure.

TINY SQUARE ENVELOPE POCKET

Perhaps all your page needs is a tiny accent of color. Here's a great tiny square envelope that can close if you want it to or remain open for a decorative pocket. The choice is yours.

Stamp: Just For Fun. Fabric: Timeless Treasures. See the Resources section, page 110.

1 Cut or tear your background fabrics to size.

2 Rubber stamp if desired.

3 Attach the background fabric to the page using spray adhesive, fusible web, or an adhesive of your choosing.

4 Fuse 2 different fabrics, wrong sides together, with fusible web.
Note: You can use glue to join the layers, but I like the extra crispness that results from using fusible web for envelopes and pockets.

5 Use a copy machine to reduce or enlarge the envelope template (page 50). Cut out your template.

6 Trace around the template and cut out your fabric envelope.

7 Hand stitch around the edge of the envelope. Continue around the flap if you choose; otherwise, complete your decorative stitches on the most visible parts of the envelope.
Note: If you prefer to machine stitch, use one of the decorative stitches available on your sewing machine to finish the edge of your envelope.

8 Fold and glue the sides and bottom of the envelope, following the folding order on the template.

9 Using heavy-duty adhesive, put glue on the back of the envelope, being careful to keep the flap free of adhesive if you want to be able to close your envelope. (If it will function as a pocket, glue the entire flap to the background.)

10 Place wax paper between the pages, close the book, and place it under some weights while the glue dries.

Martine House incorporates several fabric envelopes in her Legacy book. Her hand embroidery and beading accents are wonderful additions to the envelope flap and her impeccable handwork adds to this special family treasure.

GUM WRAPPER ENVELOPES WITH TAGS

1 Trace the gum wrapper envelope template pattern (page 50) onto paper—enlarge or reduce its size on a copy machine if necessary.

2 Trace the pattern onto freezer paper.

3 Iron the shiny side of the freezer paper onto the wrong side of the fabric.

4 Cut out the fabric and freezer paper together. Leave the freezer paper attached to add stability to the envelope.

5 Fold and glue the edges, being careful not to glue the envelope shut.

6 Place under weights or a heavy book for drying.

7 Cut purchased tags down to fit inside the envelopes, or make 1"-wide tags from cardstock.

8 Embellish tags with words or images that relate to your page. Mine say "Stamp," "Carve," and "Collage" because this spread is about that time period in my life.

9 Thread the fibers through the holes and add dangles if desired. Wait to add these small gems to your page until after you've completed the edge treatment. Otherwise, you might be stitching your envelopes closed.

10 After the page is assembled, glue your gum wrappers to the page with heavy-duty adhesive.

A recycled shirt becomes two pockets in my Travel Journal.

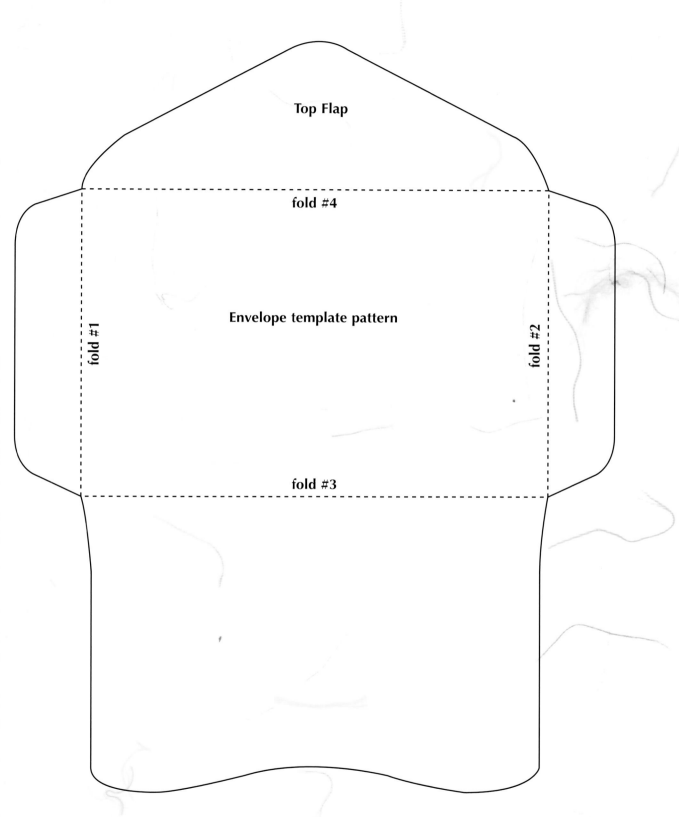

Top Flap

fold #4

Envelope template pattern

fold #1

fold #2

fold #3

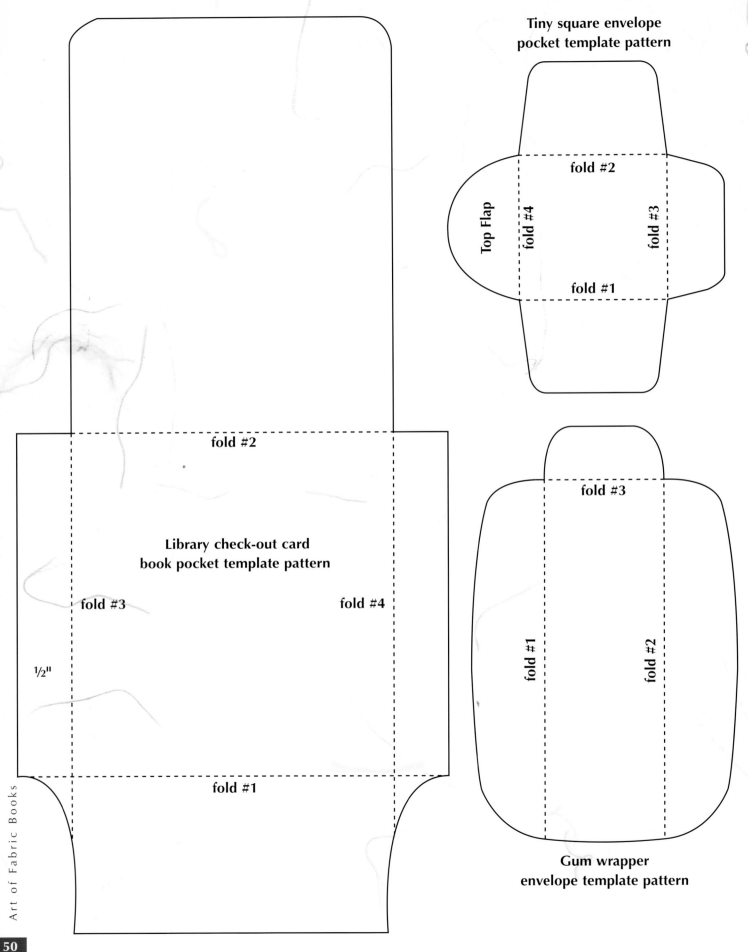

Tiny square envelope pocket template pattern

fold #2

Top Flap

fold #4

fold #3

fold #1

fold #2

Library check-out card book pocket template pattern

fold #3

fold #4

½"

fold #1

fold #3

fold #1

fold #2

Gum wrapper envelope template pattern

Text onto Pages

here are lots of ways to get text onto your pages, but here are a few ideas to get you started. The most obvious way is to write. When writing on fabric, use a marker intended for that use. Fabric markers are specifically formulated not to bleed at the edges and are available in a wide range of colors and tip widths from quilt shops and some craft stores.

Writing on fabric with a fine marker

Writing on fabric with a wide marker

Julia Slebos combined hand-written text with purchased, printed twill tape to create the text on this mini-art-quilt-page from her fabric book By the Light of the Moon.

If you don't like your handwriting, there are lots of other options.

- Use a rubber stamp alphabet to stamp what you want to say onto your book page.

- If you don't like the idea of stamping directly onto your page, consider writing or stamping onto another piece of fabric and then stitching that fabric to your page.

Kerri Lindstorm uses bold rubber stamps to stamp the title onto her altered record album.

Tip For stamping letters onto fabric, I like a nice, bold imprint. I get the best results using Versatex fabric-printing inks. See Resources (page 110).

Rubber stamp directly onto page

Kristin Steiner rubber stamped the title My Blue Book of Longing onto fabric, which she layered with other fabrics for a very effective cover. Notice the variety of letters in the word "enter."

Stamp and stitch

- If you don't want to deal with fabric edges, consider stamping on twill tape or ribbon and then stitch or glue that onto your page.

Stamping on twill tape and ribbon

- If you don't stamp, see page 27 for instructions about printing directly onto twill tape using your computer printer.

Computer printing on twill tape
and ribbon

- Paper or metal letter stencils can be used with paint to create your text. These supplies can be reused another time, or you can use the stencils themselves to spell out what you have to say.

Paper and metal stencils

Lelainia N. Lloyd stamped on twill tape to create the title for her fabric book. Every Family Has One.

Julia Slebos successfully combined printed twill tape with a metal stencil on the cover of By the Light of the Moon.

Moon Face: ARTchix collage clip sheet

Note: Some companies sell preprinted twill tape with popular words and phrases. See Resources (page 110).

■ Use leather or felt alphabets available from scrapbook and craft stores.

Leather and felt letters

■ Find vinyl, plastic, or metal letters or words to add to your pages.

Plastic, metal, and vinyl letters

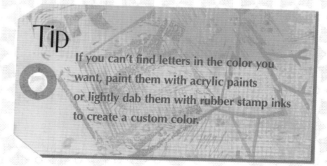

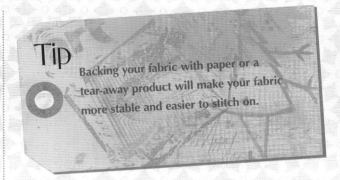

■ Dust off your embroidery floss and hand stitch letters onto your page.

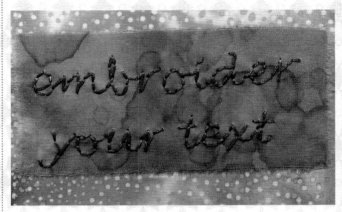

Hand embroider your text

■ Use the automatic lettering function on your sewing machine or practice your free-motion sewing machine skills and freehand your text onto the cloth.

Free-motion lettering

■ Apply fusible web to the wrong side of some fabric. Cut out your letters, either drawn freehand or traced onto the paper, then remove the paper backing and fuse them to your page.

Fuse cut letters.

■ Type your text with an old typewriter and then stitch it to your page.

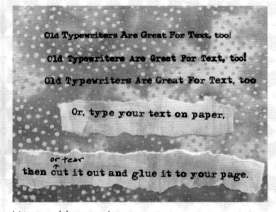

Use an old typewriter.

Tip Lightly iron the wrong side of the fabric to the shiny side of freezer paper to make it stiff enough to roll around your typewriter carriage. Type your text, then remove the fabric from the freezer paper before stitching or gluing it to your page.

■ Use your computer printer. The variety of computer fonts available is amazing. Follow the same paper preparation as indicated for typewriter printing, or use fabric specifically formulated for use with inkjet printers (see Resources on page 110).

Computer fonts

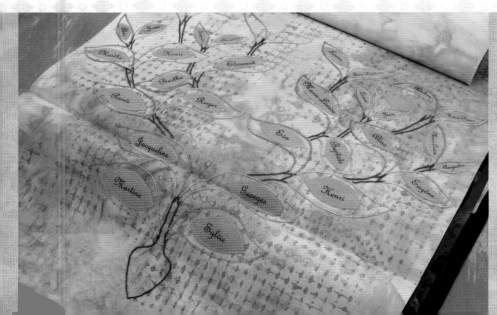

Martine House used a computer printer extensively in Legacy. Here, she printed the words for the family tree, then cut them out and appliquéd them to the background fabric.

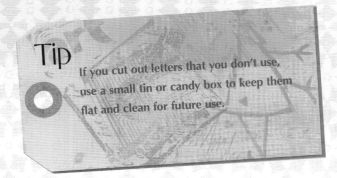

Tip

If you cut out letters that you don't use, use a small tin or candy box to keep them flat and clean for future use.

■ Use a label maker to create your text. If the sticky back on the label tape isn't strong enough to keep the text on your page, add some glue to the back of the tape. Or you could stitch the tape onto your page.

Label-maker words

Tip

Cutting text out of magazines is a great project for while you're watching television or a movie—it requires no thought while you are doing it, and you'll have a variety of text ready to use the next time you want to include some words on your pages.

■ Cut or tear and paste letters from other text. Use magazine ads, titles of articles, or junk mail text. Cut entire words, or create a ransom-note look by cutting out each letter individually to spell out your phrase.

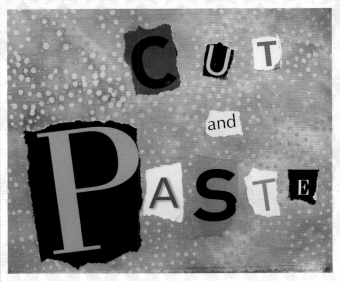

Cut and paste letters.

If you are working in an already-existing book, create "found" poetry by using the text already on the page. Simply mask, or protect, the words you want to use and paint over the rest of the page.

Highlighted words in text

A trip to a scrapbook or craft store will yield many options for text: reproduction typewriter keys, stickers, letters and words on metal eyelets, game pieces, and much more.

Buttons, metal words, and game pieces

■ Try making letters from toothpicks. Create some simple letterforms using found objects. Nails, springs, matchsticks, and wire can all be used on your pages. Also consider coins, rings, and other round objects for some letters.

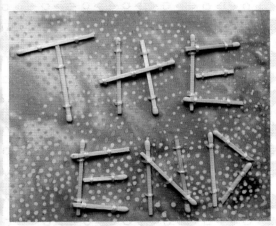

Matchstick letters

■ If you are lucky and have a thermofax machine or silk-screen supplies, they offer even more options for incorporating text into your next project.

■ When all else fails, what about stickers? And don't forget about rub-on transfers from the days before computers—remember way back then? These are fun options and very quick to apply.

Rub-on letters, tags, and stickers

One of these ideas should help you add some text onto your pages!

Tip

Masking can be achieved with removable notepad paper, low-tack masking tape, clear fingernail polish, or special masking fluid available at craft and art supply stores.

Projects

Gladys Deters

Class of 1936
Fremont High School
Fremont, Michigan

Thursday June 11
57th graduating class

ODE TO GREEN

Fabric Tag Books

Sometimes you just have to allow yourself to play. No expectations, no goals, no pressure—just pure playtime. It's important to give ourselves this special time, which can help remind us not to take ourselves too seriously. This is a perfect project for your next playtime.

My good friend Kristi Steiner told me about a fabric tag book she made. I hadn't actually seen her book, but I thought it sounded like a fun format.

I decided to start playing by focusing on texture and transfers on my tags. I thought the fabric tag book would be a great format to use as a sample book of different transfer techniques and how they work on different types of fabric.

MAKING THE FABRIC TAG BOOK

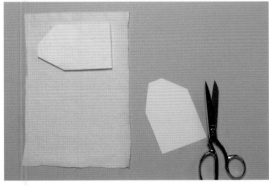

1 Cut out tag shapes from the base material. (Cut one of your fabrics large enough to fold around your tag base and cover both sides.)
Note: I cut my tags freehand because I didn't want all my tags to be exactly the same size or shape. If you want a consistent size, trace a paper tag (or the pattern on page 61) onto your base material and cut it out.

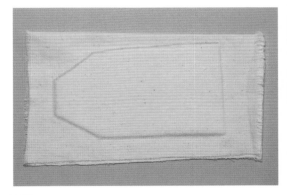

2 Machine stitch, hand stitch, fuse or glue your fabric to your tag base.
Note: I used the zipper foot on my sewing machine to sew as close as possible to the tag base.

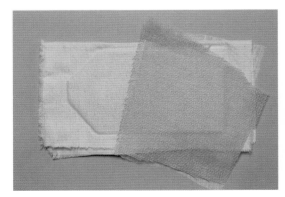

3 Overlay a different fabric onto part of the covered tag. This fabric can be parallel to the edge of the tag or at an angle. It might cover a little of the tag or a lot.

SUPPLIES

fast2fuse (a very stiff interfacing with fusible web on both sides)

Timtex (a very stiff inter-facing), **heavy interfacing**, **quilt batting**, or **paper tags** for the bases

Note: Quilt batting results in softer, more flexible tags.

Note: If you use a paper tag as your base, sew or glue fabric on top of the paper center.

Neutral-colored fabrics in a variety of textures to cover the tag base (Or, you could focus on a color family, use the same fabric to cover all your tags, or use a variety of solid colors.)

A desire to play

4 Machine stitch, hand stitch, or glue this second fabric to your tag. Repeat this process on the other side of your tag.

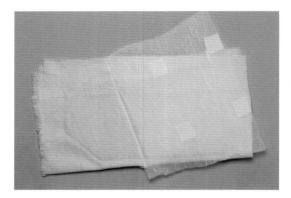

5 Sew along the edge of the overlay fabric, and sew again around the edge of the tag to include the overlay fabric in your stitches. You could use glue to hold the overlay fabric in place on your tag if you don't want to stitch it.

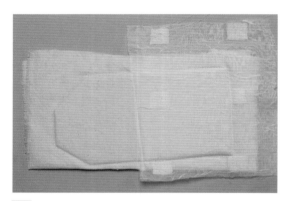

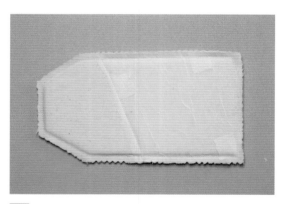

6 Trim the excess fabric from around the edges. You can use scissors or a decorative blade on your rotary cutter. Remember, there is no wrong way to play!

7 Repeat this process until you've made as many tags as you want. You can always do more later and add them to your collection.

EMBELLISHING THE TAGS

Once you have a few tags covered, think about what you can do on the surface of each fabric tag. I wanted to play with transfer techniques on top of the different textures of fabric.

If you are not interested in transfers, here are some other ideas for fabric tag playtime:

- Focus on color play. Select several fabrics from a particular color family and start building collages with snippets of cloth. Experiment with colors you don't think you like together. Colors can surprise you, so don't assume you know how two fabrics are going to look together until you've tried them.

- Found objects can be a lot of fun. Perhaps you have a collection of seashells or river rocks from a family vacation. Decorate a tag inspired by the colors of those natural objects and finish the tag by hand stitching the objects in place.

- Words can be very inspiring. Choose a few of your favorite words and decorate your tags with them. Maybe you have certain words that inspire you. Incorporate those words into your tag book and leave it in your studio to serve as a reminder of your creative energy.

- Rubber stamp onto your tags. Gather a collection of stamps and play with how they can be used to enhance one another. Maybe you've never used one as a border before, or you've always wanted to try a collage of stamp images. Here's the perfect opportunity to see what happens if . . .

- Think of yourself as a mixed-media artist. Incorporate more scraps of fabric, some collage materials, papers, or metal items. Or sew on buttons, beads, zippers, twill tape, lace, or buckles. Try playing with pattern tissue, thread, paper tags, transparencies, and sheer fabrics.

Perhaps a theme developed while you were playing with your tags, and now you have an idea for a great cover page for your fabric tag book. Maybe you prefer to keep them loose so you can play with them and shuffle them around in different combinations. Remember, there is no right or wrong way to play. Did I mention that before?

During your next playtime, you might want to add more pages to your tag book. This is a great format that encourages you to experiment with new techniques as you learn about them.

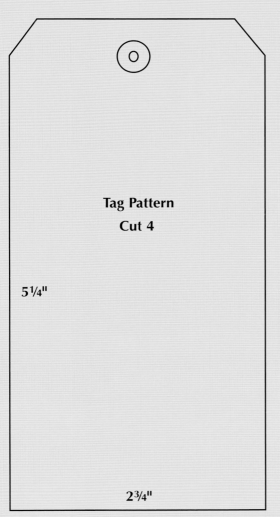

Tag Pattern

Cut 4

5¼"

2¾"

Tag template

ASSEMBLING THE FABRIC TAGS INTO A BOOK

8 Determine what order you want the tags to be— for now. You can always rearrange them.

9 Apply a large eyelet to each tag (see page 20).

10 Insert a binder ring through the eyelets to hold the fabric tag pages together.

In Secrets of My Work, *Kristin Steiner was inspired by a small book from 7 Gypsies (see Resources, page 110). She layered fabric onto paper tags, using fusible web to hold the layers together. The tags are embellished with fabric, cardstock, and even elastic printed with rubber stamps.*

In Musing, another tag book by Kristin Steiner and inspired by Suzee Gallagher, Kristi used fabric to construct the book cover and paper envelopes and tags to fill the inside. Rubber stamps and ribbon help complete Kristi's little book of wisdom.

Lelainia N. Lloyd builds Time, a fabric tag book, around a clock-theme fabric and the lyrics to Jim Croce's song "Time in a Bottle." Lelainia created this lovely tag book using paper tags, watch parts, and other embellishments.

Andrea Stern makes these assorted fabric tags while experimenting with ways to merge fabric with paper arts. Beautiful hand-dyed fabrics and stamped images are combined with other collage elements and a wonderful assortment of fibers to finish them.

Altered Board Books

Board books can be great bases for altered book projects. Typically thought of as children's books, they are easy to find and inexpensive to buy if you don't have any used ones ready to recycle. Their limited number of pages seems accessible, so you won't feel that you'll be working in it forever. If you are nervous about starting your first altered book, a board book is a great place to start. Are you already familiar with altered books? A board book is still a great choice due to the extra thickness of its pages, which easily support embellishments and mixed-media treatments.

There are a few things you need to do before beginning to alter a board book. More often than not, these books have a very durable coating to help them survive hard use. Paint and adhesives typically don't adhere well to slick surfaces. Here are three ways to prepare your board book surface to accept your artwork. Different books require different approaches. You may need to combine these techniques to prepare your board book successfully.

The objective of the following processes is to get the pages of the board book ready to accept your paint, fabric, adhesive, or whatever materials you use to alter your book.

SUPPLIES

Blank board book
(page 111)
or
Children's board book
Sandpaper
Gesso
Foam brush

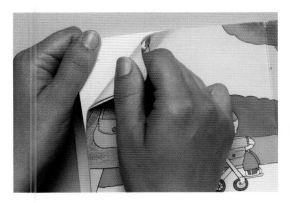

Peeling: If your board book pages have a very slick surface, simply separate the glossy topcoat from the board/cardstock and gently peel the top layer off. Typically, the book's artwork will peel off along with the glossy coating, leaving you with completely blank book pages ready for embellishment.

Sanding: If the coating on your board book does not peel off smoothly, sand the glossy finish off each page until the sheen is eliminated. I recommend doing this outdoors, because it can be messy. If the surface still feels slick after sanding, continue on to use gesso.

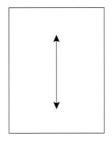 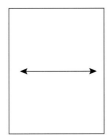

Brush in one direction, then in the other direction.

Gesso: If the board book's surface is not so slick as to require sanding (or if it's a thinner board stock), coat the pages with gesso (I like foam brushes for this). Brush on a thin layer in one direction, allow it to dry, and then apply another thin layer in the perpendicular direction.

Donna J. Engstrom takes advantage of the extra stability of a board book for Wonder. *The cover is painted, and embellished with cheesecloth, which is placed under a rusty washer that highlights the title.*

Ode to Green. *My favorite color, at least on most days, seemed to warrant a quick homage. The "new" book cover is made from fabric, embellished with rickrack, and titled with painted plastic letters.*

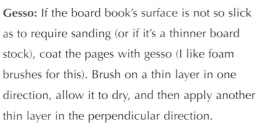

STAMP CREDITS: Specimen stamp by Stampers Anonymous; text is Jessie's Alphabet from Turtle Press

A spread from Ode to Green *illustrates my love of nature and all things green. The trading card leaf is a hand-carved stamp. I collected leaves during neighborhood walks—the perfect time to enjoy nature—dried them, and embellished them with paint.*

Wonder, *by Donna J. Engstrom, contains computer printing on muslin, which is torn and glued to painted board book pages, then embellished with buttons.*

Another fun thing about board books is finding them in interesting shapes. Corinne Stubson was inspired by the shape of this board book to create The Little Purple Pocket Book. Fabric backgrounds are enhanced with collage and, of course, purple pockets throughout this whimsical book. Notice the great bead trim on the posy pocket.

Another page from The Little Purple Pocket Book shows a triangular pocket resting on a purple bandana. The lettering was done with fabric paint.

I took advantage of the thickness of the board book pages for this clothesline page. Two fabrics create the background for the "clothesline" threaded through the eyelets. To accommodate the thickness of the small clothespins, I cut away the three pages before this page. Be careful not to cut too close to the spine or you will affect the integrity of the book. Of course, you want it to stay together. I painted the page "stubs" to blend into the fabric background and glued them together. This clothesline model would be great for a page about airing quilts, laundry day, dyed fabric samples, baby quilts, photographs, rugs, or anything else you can clip with clothespins.

Folded Fabric Books

Here's a simple, folded book project that is a lot of fun and offers endless creative possibilities. Because the book starts as one big rectangle of flat fabric (or paper), you are able to access all places on the fabric to add embellishments, stitching, layers, or whatever else you want to do before you fold the fabric into its final book format. This opens up a lot of creative potential because the book spine won't be a factor in your artistic plan.

Note: Your finished book page will be approximately one-eighth the size of the rectangle you start with. If you are making a large book, a heavier fabric is recommended. Not only will it feel better, it will result in a more stable page. It would also be fun to quilt a piece of fabric, or back your fabric with fusible interfacing or fusible batting for added strength. If you are making a smaller book, these issues require less consideration.

SUPPLIES

Rectangle of fabric or paper

Hand or machine stitching supplies or glue

MAKING THE FOLDED FABRIC BOOK

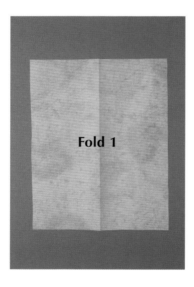

Fold 1

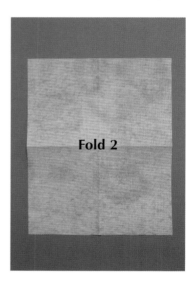

Fold 2

1 Cut or tear fabric or paper into a rectangle.

2 Fold your fabric or paper in half lengthwise to locate the center and crease.

3 Open it flat (Fold 1).

Note: If your fabric doesn't show crease lines, use pins to mark the center.

4 Fold it in half crosswise to find the center and crease.

5 Reopen it flat (Fold 2).

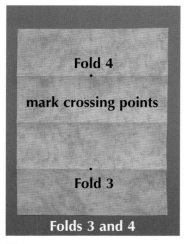

Fold 4

mark crossing points

Fold 3

Folds 3 and 4

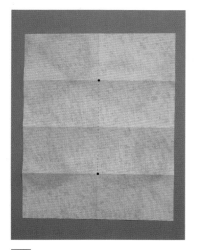

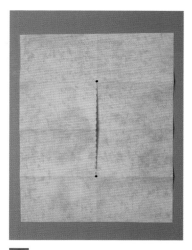

6 Fold the 2 short sides to meet in the center and crease (Folds 3 and 4).

7 Mark the point where the first fold meets these 2 side folds.

8 Reopen, with the wrong side of the fabric facing up.

9 Draw a line on the center of the first fold, stopping at fold marks 3 and 4.

10 Cut a slit on the dotted line.

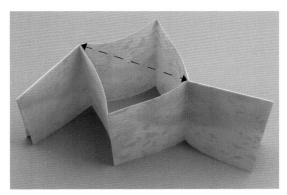

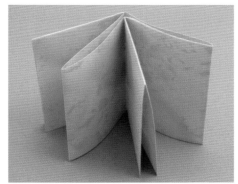

11 Open out along the fold, wrong sides together.

12 Close to create your book pages. Re-crease or iron as necessary to make it as flat as possible.

Mark the page numbers to help you keep track of which spread is which while you sew, add transfers, and otherwise embellish your book. Collage, stitch, paint, or otherwise decorate your fabric book pages, staying away from the folds, so your book will close flat. When all the pages are complete, refold the book and enjoy!

Note: If you don't want to leave the fabric edges raw, see pages 35–38 for some finishing options.

My Coffee Book

In By the Light of the Moon *by Julia Slebos, Julia covered the raw edges of her fabric pages with a separate piece of background fabric. She mitered the corners to simulate a picture frame.*

For Hear, *Gabe Cyr folded her fabric pages, completed the artwork, then inserted the pages into the existing hard covers of a gutted book. See the "Scrapbook/Journal" project (page 71) for more information about this process.*

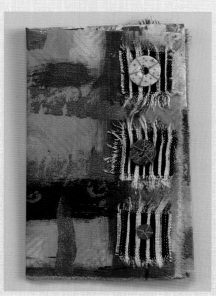

Gabe Cyr's folded fabric book Daylight Crescendo *includes shells, polymer clay, beads, and paper.*

Gabe Cyr's folded fabric Wind Haiku *book includes metal and wood elements.*

Fabric Books

You may often hear that a successful fiction writer merely writes about what he or she knows: life experience. Well, should it be any different for a visual artist? I didn't think so either, so I made the fabric book *How I Got Here*. You obviously got to this point in your life on a different path, so your story is different from mine. Enjoy the process, remember creative milestones, and document your artistic endeavors along the way.

If you are not interested in illustrating your creative background, consider making a fabric book about a recent trip, for a young child*, to illustrate your love of gardening, about (or for!) someone special, to create a tactile reminder of a special day, or to play with color. There is no limit to the ideas you can execute in fabric.

*If you are making a book for a young child, be very mindful of the embellishments you use. Secure all buttons well and avoid using small objects that could pop off.

MAKE THE PAGES

1 Tear or cut your fabric pages to size and decorate them to your satisfaction. Add to the stability of lighter-weight fabrics by backing them with quilt batting, fast2fuse (page 111), Timtex, or other stiff material.

2 Finish the edges of the pages. Refer to the suggestions about fabric edge finishes in the Techniques section (page 35) for some easy methods.

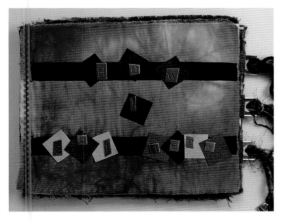

ASSEMBLING THE BOOK

1 Cut pieces of twill tape or ribbon at least 3" longer than your book cover is wide.

2 Pin twill tape in place on the front cover.

3 With hand or machine stitches, stitch the twill tape onto the cover, stopping about 1" from the left edge.

4 Mark and sew buttonholes near the left edge of your cover. Be sure the holes are long enough to accommodate your twill or ribbon.

5 Use the location of the buttonholes on the cover as the template for marking buttonholes on the other pages.

6 After all the buttonholes are sewn, thread the twill tape through all the holes in page order, front to back.

7 On the back of the book, thread the twill tape through the buckles and stitch the twill tape so the buckles can't come loose.

SUPPLIES

Fabric: I use a variety of hand-dyed and overdyed fabrics, but choose fabrics that will support **your** theme.

Quilt batting, **fast2fuse** (page 111), **Timtex**, or other base for your pages

Thread for machine or hand stitching

Glue, fusible web, or spray adhesive

Twill tape or ribbon

Hand or machine stitching supplies

Two buckles

Completed fabric doll page

Stamp credit:
Jessie's Alphabet from Turtle Press

A string of fabric "paper" dolls, embellishments and stamped text complete this fabric doll page.

AB page

Stamps, fabric, game pieces, eyelet tape, paper, and more were used to create this spread illustrating my adventure into the world of altered books.

Quilts page

A miniature quilt block, photos of my quilts, and mini show ribbons combine to illustrate my love of quilting.

Back cover

I couldn't resist making a "real" About the Author page for the back cover of How I Got Here. Stamped twill, a carved self-portrait printed on pattern tissue, and my grandmother's buttons all come together for the final page.

Scrapbook/Journal

This book is so much fun to make. You'll amaze yourself with what you can create. It starts as a cast-off hardcover book and is transformed into your scrapbook/journal. We'll add fabric pockets, paper embellishments, and lots more. Choose a book whose size and shape you like so you can get started!

Mine is a travel journal, but here are some other themes that would be perfect to use when following this step-by-step process to create an original book:

- Gardening
- Quilting journal
- Wedding album
- Family scrapbook

- Honoring family pets
- Family recipe book
- Documenting your genealogy research
- Creating a new book annually to document your child's school year

GUTTING THE BOOK

The first thing to do is remove the pages from the book. Throw them away or use them in future collage, altered book, or scrapbook projects. It's a simple process, so don't stop now.

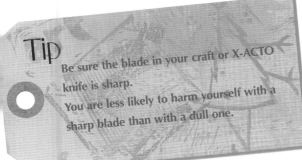

Tip
Be sure the blade in your craft or X-ACTO knife is sharp.
You are less likely to harm yourself with a sharp blade than with a dull one.

1 Open the book and carefully cut the end paper between the front cover and the book spine.

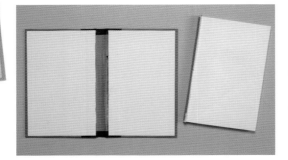

2 Repeat this process at the back of the book, and completely remove the pages from the book.

SUPPLIES

Hardbound book—don't worry about the condition of the pages; they'll be removed

Fabrics and **papers**

Tyvek or **cloth tape**

Tip: This is a great chance to recycle a used mailing envelope (some Priority Mail and FedEx envelopes are made of Tyvek).

Glue

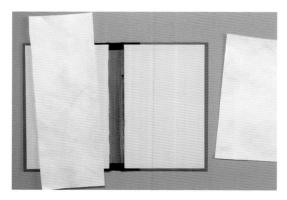

3 Lay the empty book cover flat on the table.

4 Measure the height and width of your book spine.

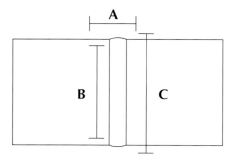

Measuring your book spine

5 Cut 2 strips of Tyvek, cloth tape, or other tear-resistant material. Cut both strips the width of your book spine plus 3" (A). Cut one piece about 1/2" shorter than the height of your book spine (B). Cut the other piece about 3" longer than the height of your book spine (C).

6 Glue the shorter piece of Tyvek inside the book and use a bone folder or the back of a spoon to secure it to the book. This step ensures good contact between your reinforcing material and the book spine.

7 Glue the longer piece of Tyvek to the outside of the book spine, wrapping the excess around to the inside and overlapping the inside piece.

8 Secure this piece and set the cover aside.

MAKING THE PAGES FOR INSIDE THE BOOK

Don't limit yourself to only the ideas shown in this sample project. You can use fabric pages, paper ephemera, envelopes, pockets, plastic collection bags sewn onto paper, travel maps, postage stamps, travel advertisements . . . there really is no limit! It's easy to access the pages because they aren't sewn into the book yet. Hand or machine stitch or glue the items onto your pages.

9 Make enough pages to lightly fill the space, but keep in mind that you will be adding treasures that will add bulk. The largest you can make your pages is the height of the book cover (less about 1/4") times twice the finished page width. This size will allow you to sew down the center of your pages to hold them into your book.

IDEAS FOR YOUR BOOK

Be sure to include some pockets or envelopes for collecting items. These can be paper envelopes that you stitch or glue to your page or fabric envelopes that you make (see pages 39–50 for pocket and envelope ideas).

Pocket pages are great for:

- Adding cropped (trimmed) photos

- Printing out your itinerary and putting a page a day in your pockets

- Collecting items of interest on your trip

- Making an impromptu collage of items found along the way

- Displaying paint chips that remind you of the colors of your destination

- Notes about favorite sites along the journey

- Words you overheard at a particular spot

- Comments your kids made about a place

Not all of the pages have to cross the entire width of your book. As long as they cross the centerline and can be stitched into your book, they'll work fine. You might want to include some "shorter" widths for interest. These short pieces are also great places to add tags, pockets, and envelopes.

Short page with library check-out card pocket

I love a combination of textures, so I enjoy mixing paper, fibers, metal, fabrics, and whatever else is within reach. This is a great project for incorporating a wide variety of materials. Enjoy!

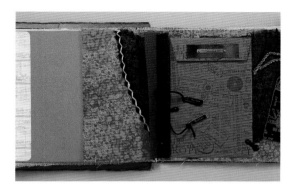

Optional: When you have your pages ready to sew into your book, machine stitch down the center of the pages to help hold them together. If you have a fragile center page, consider adding a strip of cardstock to reinforce your center stitching. Travel stamp by Just For Fun.

COVERING THE BACK AND SPINE OF THE BOOK

To complete your reconstructed book, you'll probably want to cover the back and spine with fabric that supports your theme. This is a simple process, but make sure you allow adequate time for the adhesive to dry.

Inside of Book

1 Cut a piece of fabric approximately 3" taller than your book. Cut it wide enough to allow about 1½" to wrap to the inside on the back and long enough to wrap completely around the spine and onto the front of your book.

Outside of Book

2 Spread adhesive thoroughly onto the back and spine of your book.

3 Apply the fabric to the adhesive.

4 Then, use the heel of your hand, bone folder, or back of a large spoon to gently rub it, making sure that there is good contact in all areas.

5 Spread adhesive on the inside of the book covers where the fabric will wrap around. Extend the adhesive farther than your fabric to ensure it stays secure.

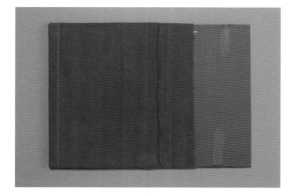

6 Wrap the excess fabric around to the inside of your book cover. Smooth into place and let dry completely.

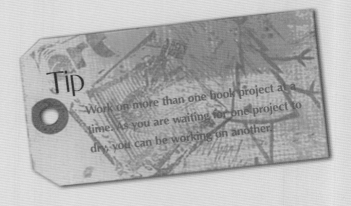

Tip

Work on more than one book project at a time. As you are waiting for one project to dry, you can be working on another.

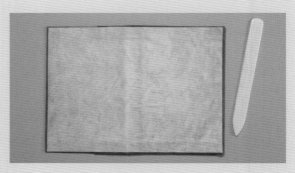

7 Cut a piece of paper to fit the entire inside of the cover.

8 Spread adhesive all around inside the cover.

9 Position the paper and use the heel of your hand, bone folder, or back of a large spoon to gently rub it, making sure that there is good contact in all areas. Allow to dry completely.

BINDING THE BOOK AND ADDING THE FRONT COVER

If you have never bound a book before, don't worry. It's not difficult at all. Just a few simple steps and you'll be finished. Really.

SUPPLIES

Covered book (front cover still detached)

Hole punch

Block of pages ready to sew into your book

Ribbon, yarn, or cord to sew book together

Hand-sewing needle appropriate for your cord

Decorated cover

Eyelets and setting tools (optional)

Any embellishments, beads, or charms you want to dangle from the spine

SEWING THE BOOK TOGETHER

1 Measure the height of your book spine.

2 Decide how many holes you want to make, considering that an odd number of holes will look better than an even number. I chose to make 5 holes. Space the holes evenly. Use a piece of scrap paper to make a template to mark the location of the holes.

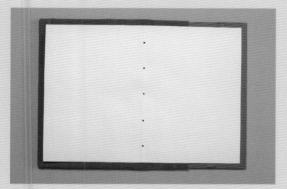

3 Use your template and a hole punch to punch the holes all the way through the binding, fabric, and inside paper. Optional: Add eyelets and eyelet washers to the binding holes in your book spine.

4 Use this same template paper to repeat the punching process on your block of pages.

5 Stack pages one on top of the other. Place your block of pages inside your book cover and line up the holes.

6 Cut a piece of cord (or bookbinding thread, or whatever you are using to sew your book together) approximately three times longer than the length of the binding.

7 Start sewing inside the book if you want the tails to end up inside your book. If you want to dangle charms, beads, or other items from the spine of your book, start sewing from the outside of the spine.

8 Sew following the pattern below. The pattern will be the same for any odd number of holes. Option: Add beads between each of the holes for extra embellishment on the spine of your book.

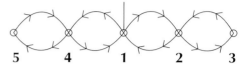

Start here/end here

5   4   1   2   3

Book sewing diagram

9 Adjust the tension of your thread after you finish sewing, making sure the book block is securely in place.

10 Tie a square knot to hold the ends together. If you started your thread on the inside, you can trim the thread tails after knotting. If you started with your thread on the outside, you can add charms, beads, and other dangles before knotting the ends to secure the beads.

11 Glue the decorated cover to the front of your book and enjoy!

Completed cover

Completed project

Altered Scrapbook

We spent a lot of time with Aunt Gladys when we were growing up. She didn't have any children of her own, so she seemed to enjoy entertaining nieces and nephews. Playing games at the cottage, going blueberry picking, hosting family picnics—the perfect jobs for an aunt. After Aunt Gladys died, we sorted through some photographs, and this scrapbook is the result. Aunt Gladys was a bookkeeper, so I chose a ledger/journal for the book to alter.

Rather than go step-by-step through the process of creating every page, I'll attempt to point out unique processes or highlights. After all, you can't possibly have exactly the same stuff to put into your scrapbook, so it's the *process* that is the most important. Gather a favorite family member's memorabilia and start your tribute to his or her life.

SUPPLIES

A book to alter or a blank scrapbook to use as your foundation

THE COVER

If you are going to be adding fragile or three-dimensional items to the cover, I suggest waiting until the end of your project to apply them.

Cover; purchased bead trim

I chose the sheer fabric for the cover for two reasons. One, I like the way it looks with the blouse Aunt Glad is wearing in the photograph. Two, I like the way the vintage ledger/journal cover shows through the fabric.

The photograph is a copy onto linen fabric prepared for inkjet printing (see the Resources section, page 110).

The library check-out card on the Dedication Page is included so family members can sign it after they've had a chance to see the book.

To celebrate her life, I included the following sections in my scrapbook:

Dedication page; scrapbook papers, library card pocket embellished with dye inks and painted drywall tape.

Baby page; photocopy onto linen prepared for inkjet printing (see Resources page 110), dye inks sponged onto background, satin photo corners and Ultra suede frame around text printed on transparency.

Slanted pocket page (page 44) to hold:

- Extra photos

- Handwritten letters

- Recipe cards from someone special

- Invitations to events

- Travel brochures

- Playbills from special shows

- Tickets and receipts from travel

- Tags embellished with a theme

- Coasters from favorite restaurants

- Postcards

Slanted pocket pages; the perfect place to hold treasured photographs.

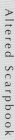

Graduation day; photo was inkjet printed onto a transparency, sheer fabric background attached with eyelets, layered papers, vintage doily, and an embellished tag for additional interest.

A Pocketful of Memories; vintage dresser scarves, rub on letters, and copies of photos.

WWII; Army pants rescued from the thrift store served the foundation for this spread. The pockets create more space for letters, photos, etc.

The Wedding day; painted mesh fabric, hand stitching and a copy of the marriage license.

Family gathering at Sand Lake; sheer black fabric, mesh paper, captions from an old label maker, and clock fabric support the photos.

The Cottage; retro kitchen fabric, sticky (self-adhesive) rickrack, and computer printed text and photos are combined in this spread.

Fabric: Michael Miller Fabrics

Pink Poodle pet page; cotton fabric, polka dot ribbon, plastic letters, rickrack and rhinestone trim to simulate a dog collar.

Michael Miller Fabrics

Game collage; a terrific fabric supports miscellaneous game pieces to remember Aunt Gladys' love of playing games.

Michael Miller Fabrics

Retirement day; 7 Gypsies number paper, layered with a copy of the newspaper article.

Paper: 7 Gypsies

I hope these altered scrapbook pages about my Aunt Gladys will inspire you to create a scrapbook about someone you love. Find a book with content that relates to the person, or start with a blank scrapbook as your base. Either way, you'll enjoy the memories while you create, as well as for many years to come.

The Couples satin photo corners lovingly hold photos of a couple married for over 50 years.

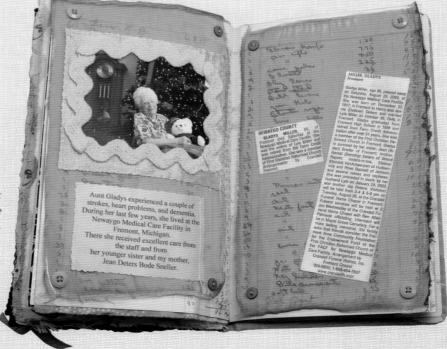

Special photos; sheer fabric allows the ledger entries to be seen behind the photo and text.

Gallery

■ Beads, Buttons, Ribbons, and Lace were used beautifully by Andrea Stern to embellish the cover of her fabric book *Mom-Mom and Me,* in honor of her paternal grandmother.

■ Beads, Buttons, and Findings were used by Juliana Coles to patch together fabrics from a trip to India as she fashioned her visual journal *Don't Turn Away* in an altered 1940s photo album.

■ A Tea Towel and Upholstery Trim are wonderful additions to the cover of Linda Harral's small altered book *Gardens*.

■ Ribbons, Charms, a Dishtowel, and Vintage Items adorn the simple cover of *The Virgin of Guadalupe,* an altered book by Sandra Ahlgren Sapienza.

■ Rayon Fabric, Organza Ribbon, Buttons, and Decorative Machine Stitching make Kristi Schueler's cover appealing.

■ Layered Fabric, Photo Transfer, and Hand Stitching adorn the cover of Andrea Stern's layered cloth cover for *Piece of My Heart*.

■ Cheesecloth, Part of a Thread Spool, Yarn, Buttons, Paint, and more were used to create this cover from *A Common Thread* by Diana L. Klimt-Perenick.

■ Lettering and Stitching come together on the title page of Joyce M.A. Gary's altered book *Juxtaposition*. The book is an ongoing exploration that combines her varied interests while comparing and contrasting differences.

■ Beads, Buttons, Findings, and Dimensional Elements come together on this quilted book cover by Lenna Andrews Foster, which she began in a class with Keely Barham.

■ Paint and Stitching were used by Karen Michel for the cover of *Uncover Your Story, 2.0.*

■ Paint, Fabric, Embroidery, Beadwork, Stamps, and Mesh were used by Joyce M.A. Gary for this wonderful page spread in *Juxtaposition*.

■ Painted Gesso, Heavy Gel Medium, Paint, Glaze, and Yarn were used on this spread from *Juxtaposition* by Joyce M.A. Gary. The stitched twisted yarns on the right side were used to mimic the left side.

■ Xpandaprint (paint that expands when heat is applied), Acrylic Paints, Free-Motion Machine Quilting, and Hand Stitching come together on this alligator spread from *Juxtaposition*. The painted fabric was free-motion machine quilted before Joyce M.A. Gary hand stitched it to the book page, where she highlighted the text about alligators.

■ Handmade Paper, Dried Flowers, Polymer Clay, Tree Bark, and Free-Motion Machine Embroidery adorn this spread in *Juxtaposition* by Joyce M.A. Gary.

■ Donna J. Engstrom combined Pattern Tissue, Beads, Her Daughter's Poetry, Vintage Jewelry, and a Niche (cut out, recessed area) in this spread in her altered book *She*.

■ Paint, Tape, Stitched Paper, Photographs, and Ephemera helped Juliana Coles create her artist book *Bad Manners: Love, Desire, and the Female Body*. This evocative mixed media work appears in an altered 1918 psychology book.

■ Bark and Hand Stitching
are the elements used in
Kerrie E. Carbary's *Field Book
of Rocks and Minerals.*

■ Lace was used as the root
system for the tree in this altered
book, *Making Things Grow,*
by Kerrie E. Carbary.

■ Tumbled Glass and Hand Stitching allow Kerrie E. Carbary to explore a variety of mediums in her altered book *Field Book of Rocks and Minerals*.

■ Paper Pulp over a Mesh Base, Paint, and Stitching with Hemp Thread are combined into a swirl in *Making Things Grow* by Kerrie E. Carbary.

■ Painted Canvas, Watercolor Paper, Silk Ribbon, Machine Stitching, and Image Transfers are all combined in Andrea Stern's book *Doll Baby, Sugar Lamb.*

■ Gabe Cyr combined Hand-Painted Fabric, Commercial Batik, Stenciled Text, and more in this spread from *Hear.*

■ Rubber Stamps, Stitching, and Pattern Tissue tie together sewing elements in Julia Slebos's *19th Century Babes*. Stamps by Acey Deucy, Catherine Moore, and Post Modern Design.

■ Paint Chip Cards, Stitching, Handwriting, and Rubber Stamps were combined by Julia Slebos to create this spread, "A Waist is a Terrible Thing to Mind," in *Sew It Seems*. Stamps by Stampers Anonymous, Hot Potatoes, and Acey Deucy.

■ Appliqué, Found Objects, Beads, and more contribute to the success of this spread in Andrea Stern's book *Mom-Mom and Me.*

■ Paint on Collaged Paper and Fancy Trim set off this page of Juliana Coles's visual journal *Broken: Big Book III 1996–2000.*

■ Constructed Minature Kimonos and Japanese Paper Frames were used in Delores Hamilton's book.

■ Fabric, Japanese Paper and Hand Beading are framed inside the cover by Delores Hamilton in *Ceremonial Kimonos.*

■ Lettering, Buttons, and Findings can be found in this spread from *Every Family Has One* by Lelainia N. Lloyd, which honors the family hero.

THE HERO HAS AN INNATE SENSE OF RIGHT AND WRONG AND FIGHTS ON THE SIDE OF JUSTICE. THIS PERSON UPHOLDS THE IDEALS OF COURAGE, LOYALTY, INTEGRITY AND HONOUR AND THEIR LIVES BECOME LEGENDARY.

■ Crochet, Appliqué, Buttons, and More are combined successfully in Andrea Stern's *Mom-Mom and Me.*

■ Buttons and Lace were used by Carol Owen as both overlay and frame for this spread in *Bingo.*

■ Lace can be used in many different ways, including as a tree trunk in Kerrie E. Carbary's *Making Things Grow*.

■ Lace and Hand Stitching are combined by Joyce M.A. Gary for this spread in *Juxtaposition*.

■ Buttons, Paper, and Fabric—can you tell which are real and which are copies in this spread by Joyce M.A. Gary in *Juxtaposition?*

■ Buttons, Denim, and Hand Stitching form this spread in Diana K. Klimt-Perenick's altered book *A Common Thread.*

■ Slide Holders (cut from paper), Vintage Buttons, Snaps, and Rubber Stamps combine in Julia Slebos's *Sew It Seems*. Stamps by Stampers Anonymous, PSX, and Catherine Moore.

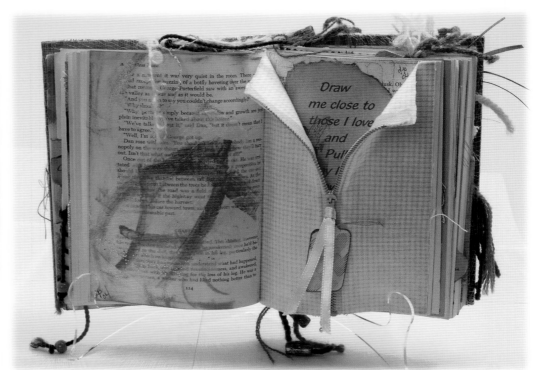

■ A Zipper opens to reveal text in *A Common Thread* by Diana K. Klimt-Perenick.

■ Gel Transfers, Hand Stitching, Paint, and Zippers are combined in *In Measure: The Sun Proceeds Unmoved* by Jen Worden.

■ Appliqué, Reverse Appliqué, and Stitching in a partially completed quilt from a workshop with David Walker are turned into book pages for both sides of Carol Owen's *Seasons of the Moon* accordion book.

■ Letters, Lace, Trim, and Buttons highlight this accordion book, *My Mother—Myself,* by Lenna Andrews Foster, which was partially completed in a Lesley Riley workshop.

■ Paper, paint, printing, and two books were used to create Corinne Stubson's sculpture *The Voice of the Artist Cannot Be Silenced.*

■ Layered Cheesecloth, Paint, and Paper were the elements S. Zoe Hecht used in *Failure is Impossible,* which was inspired by Susan B. Anthony and the suffrage movement.

■ Fabric, Jewelry, Paper, Shells, and more are combined by Corinne Stubson in the niche (cut out, recessed area) of *Botticelli Revisited.*

■ Vintage Pattern Pieces, Hooks and Eyes, Rickrack, Tape Measures, and more are all part of this fun spread in Kerri Lindstrom's *Notions* altered record album sleeve.

■ Paper Tags, Lace, Rubber Stamps, and Zippers are included on this spread in *Notions* by Kerri Lindstrom.

■ Paper Collage was used by Lelainia N. Lloyd to create two terrific custom daytimers: *Angel of Lost Buttons* and *A Woman's Hands.*

■ Pattern Tissue, Vintage Snaps, Rickrack, and Trim form the perfect combination for this page from Kerri Lindstrom's *Notions* altered record album sleeve.

■ Fiber Art and Digital Images were collaged as loose pages in Randy Keenan's compositions, *Anchors A' Weigh* (top left), *Spirit* (top right), *Faster Than a Rabbit* (bottom left), and *Hung by Her Purse* (bottom right).

■ Rescued Library CD Boxes, Fabric, Paint, Paper, Glue, Hand Stitching, Collage, Beads, and more come together to create Carol Vasenko's original "Journal Boxes" (these two pages). Inside each box is a "quiltlet"—a small quilt.

■ Appliqué, Beading, Hand and Machine Embroidery, Photo Transfer, and Text (printed from the computer directly onto fabric) are combined by Martine House to create this masterpiece fabric book, *Legacy*, (these two pages) to honor her family and record information for future generations.

■ Photo Transfer, Text, and Embroidery come together in closed, then opened, *Legacy*.

■ Velvet and Beading highlight the fabulous cover of Martine House's *Legacy*.

■ Fabric, Decorative Machine Stitches, and Hooks and Eyes were used by Kristi Schueler to make this great little "booklace"—a book that's a necklace, so you're never caught without paper to jot down a note or phone number.

Contributing Artists

Kerrie E. Carbary
Seattle, Washington
www.dogearedmagazine.com

Juliana Coles
Albuquerque, New Mexico
www.meandpete.com

Gabe Cyr
Asheville, North Carolina
www.gabecyr.com

Donna J. Engstrom
Brighton, Michigan
www.thecreativeside.com

Lenna Andrews Foster
East Granby, Connecticut
www.lennastamp.com

Joyce A. Gary
Atlanta, Georgia
jmag50@aol.com

Delores Hamilton
Cary, North Carolina

Linda Harral
Anderson, South Carolina

S. Zoe Hecht
Brooklyn, New York
www.itsmysite.com/parsifalsSister

Martine Caillon House
www.housefiber.com

Randy Keenan
Caldwell, New Jersey
keenanr@eclipse.net

Diana Klimt-Perenick
Wisconsin
http://myweb.core.com/photos/
    perenick@vbe.com

Kerri Lindstrom
Nampa, Idaho
artgirl30@yahoo.com

Lelainia N. Lloyd
British Columbia, Canada
http://members.shaw.ca/tatterededge

Karen Michel
Long Beach, New York
www.karenmichel.com

Carol Owen
www.carolowenart.com

Sandra Ahlgren Sapienza
Crownsville, Maryland
www.needlearts-adventures.com

Kristi Schueler
Fort Collins, Colorado
www.kurki15.com

Julia Slebos
Durham, North Carolina

Jan Bode Smiley
Fort Mill, South Carolina
www.jansmiley.com

Kristin Steiner
Columbia, South Carolina
kbsteiner@surfbest.net

Andrea Stern
Chauncey, Ohio
www.embellishmentcafe.com

Corinne Stubson
Medford, Oregon
http://www.glitz-oh.com

Carol Vasenko
Newark, Ohio

Jen Worden
Wentzell Lake, Nova Scotia, Canada
www.jenworden.com

Index

Product Information

ALTERED BOOKS

International Society of Altered Book Artists
www.alteredbookartists.com/index.html

Altered Book Group
http://groups.yahoo.com/group/alteredbooks

Tom Phillips Amazing Altered Book
www.humument.com

OTHER ON-LINE RESOURCES

Copyright Information for Collage Artists
www.funnystrange.com/copyright

Translations of words and phrases into other languages
http://world.altavista.com

FABRICS

Color Textiles

Cotton and linen fabrics prepared to print on inkjet printers
www.Colortextiles.com

Robert Kaufman Fabrics
Jennifer Sampou Color Rhythm fabrics

Lonni Rossi Fabric Design Studio & Store
Typospheres cotton fabrics
www.LonniRossi.com

Michael Miller Fabrics
Great retro-theme fabrics
www.michaelmillerfabrics.com

Paris Flea Market Fabric by 3 Sisters for Moda Fabrics
www.modafabrics.com

Timeless Treasures Fabrics
www.ttfabrics.com

PAPER AND OTHER SUPPLIES

All My Memories
www.allmymemories.com

Colorbök
Self-adhesive rickrack, satin photo corners, stitched envelopes
www.colorbok.com

The Paper Loft, LLC
Incredible papers and alphabet stickers
www.paperloft.com

7 Gypsies
Printed twill tape, interesting papers, journal hardware, lots more
www.7gypsies.com

RUBBER STAMPS

The Turtle Press
Jessie's Letter alphabet and other great
rubber stamp alphabets
www.turtlearts.com

Just For Fun
Rubber stamps
www.jffstamps.com

MaVinci's Reliquary
Incredible variety of rubber stamp alphabets
http://crafts.dm.net/mall/reliquary

Stampington & Company
www.stampington.com

OTHER RECOMMENDED PRODUCTS

3-in-1 Color Tool
To help select color schemes
www.ctpub.com

Blank Board Books
www.ctpub.com

Easels
To display your books
www.easels.com

fast2fuse
Stiff interfacing with fusible web on both sides
www.ctpub.com

Golden Paints and Mediums
www.goldenpaints.com

Jo Sonja's Paints
www.josonjas.com

Junkitz
Self-adhesive zippers, great buttons,
and alphabet buttons
www.junkitz.com

Kreinik Threads
Iron-on threads
www.kreinik.com

Quilters Dream Batting
Batting
www.quiltersdreambatting.com

The Stamp Peddler
Japanese screw punch
www.stamppeddler.com

Versatex
Printing inks
www.jacquardproducts.com

Journey

About the Author

Jan Smiley is an author and mixed media artist. She began her artistic life as a quiltmaker, and took those skills with her as she crossed over into book arts, where she takes great pleasure in merging the mediums.

First carving her own stamps for use on paper and fabric, then learning about altered books, visual journals, and scrapbooks, she enjoys exploring the unlimited potential of combining her interests.

Discover

Vacation

Hear the whispers of my heart...